D1293508

BY PAUL HORGAN

JOSIAH GREGG
AND HIS VISION OF
THE EARLY WEST

JOSIAH GREGG

This daguerreotype is his only known portrait

JOSIAH GREGG AND HIS VISION OF THE EARLY WEST

Paul Horgan

FARRAR STRAUS GIROUX

NEW YORK

Library of Congress Cataloging in Publication Data
Horgan, Paul.
Josiah Gregg and his vision of the early West.
Bibliography: p.
Includes index.
1. Gregg, Josiah, 1806–1850.
2. Southwest, New—Description and travel.
3. Mexico—Description and travel.
4. Gregg, Josiah, 1806–1850. Commerce of the prairies.
5. Pioneers—Southwest, New—Biography.
I. Title.
F800.G74H67   976'.03'0924   79–13081

For
Bob and Barbara
in their
Circle Diamond
Library

CONTENTS

JOSIAH GREGG
AND HIS VISION OF
THE EARLY WEST

PREFACE

T HIS BOOK BRINGS TOGETHER IN CONTINU-
ity various studies of Josiah Gregg which I published
earlier in separate form. These were originally stimulated by
the historical research of Colonel Maurice Garland Fulton, late
professor of English in the New Mexico Military Institute,
where we were colleagues.

Little or nothing was known of Gregg, even after his famous
book, *Commerce of the Prairies*, was published in 1844. It was
a trail-breaking work in the historiography of the American West
which remains a classic. In scholarly pursuit of him, Fulton, in
the 1930s, discovered clues which led him to descendants of the
Gregg family, and thus to documents which completed the
story of Gregg's life.

Examining volumes of local history in Kansas City, Fulton
came across allusions to one Claude Hardwicke, who was said
to possess manuscript diaries and other writings of Gregg, some
of which had been used in the making of *Commerce of the
Prairies*. Tracing the Hardwicke family, Fulton found Mr
Claude Hardwicke, a bedridden invalid, in Independence, Missouri. And who was he? The grandnephew of Gregg. Did he
have these papers? He did. When Claude Hardwicke was a
boy, he used to climb up to the attic of his family's house in In-

3

dependence, and there he would read in fascination about life on the Western prairies, in words by the man who best of all described it.

Both Hardwicke and his wife placed the highest historical value on the papers, and American history is their debtor for so faithfully keeping them. They permitted Fulton to examine the manuscripts, among which he found portions of *Commerce of the Prairies* in immediate, on-the-spot entries of the diaries; and there, too, polished, orderly, corrected, was the series of notebooks marked MSS 2, 3, 4, and 5, to which Josiah's brother John evidently gave the title *Rovings Abroad*. These items comprised a completed work, carrying Gregg from September 1846 to August 1849. They described what he saw and did in the Republics of Texas and Mexico. He said of this manuscript that he "expected to publish within a year."

This never came about. Before Gregg went to California in 1849, on the last expedition from which he never returned, he left his literary materials with agents in San Francisco whom he instructed to send them to his brother John if not reclaimed. So it was that after his death his unpublished book found its way to John Gregg in Louisiana, and so the possession came down through the family, giving us Gregg's later life up to the point of the California venture.

For the story of his last days we have recourse to a newspaper account published six years later by a survivor of the expedition. This was L. K. Wood, of Mason County, Kentucky.

The Gregg notebooks, diaries, and letters to his family and to newspaper editors, along with L. K. Wood's account of the California ordeal, appeared together in *Diary and Letters of Josiah Gregg:* Volume One, Southwestern Enterprises, 1840–1847, and Volume Two, Excursions in Mexico and California, 1847–1850, both edited by Maurice Garland Fulton, and published by the University of Oklahoma Press (Norman) in 1941 and 1944 respectively. Colonel Fulton's full bibliographical appara-

tus can be seen in these volumes. Drawing on their materials, I
wrote introductory essays to both which were divided between
them, under the inclusive title *Josiah Gregg Himself*. In revised
form, they appear in this book as Parts I, III, and IV. Part II
consists of an interpretation of *Commerce of the Prairies* which I
published in *Southwest Review* in 1941 under the title "The
Prairies Revisited: A Re-estimation of Josiah Gregg," which is
now revised for its place in the continuity of the present volume.
Thanks are due to the original publishers for permission to put
my materials to their new use here.

In preparing my comments on *Commerce of the Prairies* I
used the following editions of the work: New York, Henry
Langley, 1844; Dallas, The Southwest Press, 1933; and Norman, The University of Oklahoma Press, 1954, the definitive
modern edition, admirably edited by Max L. Moorhead.

INTRODUCTION

WHETHER IN ROMANCE OR FACT, THE SUBject of the American West remains inexhaustible. In 1871, an old man, a pioneer of Kansas City, was recalling for an audience drawn from his own generation what it was that excited everyone so when they were so young.

"Colonel Bartleson, Governor Boggs, Joab Powell," recited our witness, "Jim Baxter, Tom Rule, and a host of the first pioneers of this region, long years ago chased that vanishing phantom land over the Western plains, the snowy range, the Sierra Nevadas, and lost sight of it forever in the broad Pacific.

"In early youth we removed and settled in a country universally known as the 'Great West' . . . All of the vast territory almost unknown and untraveled, lying from the Mississippi westward to the Pacific Ocean, was once known as the 'Great West.' Towns, steamboats, post offices, and children, were named 'Far West' in honor of that wonderful country—but where is that famous land today [1871]? Even the name is unused and unknown."

For most men their daily imperatives lie in the present. But now and then a single creature holds fast, like an eternal boy, to the desires and trappings of the long ago; and is turned into a caricature simply by the passing of time.

"Only one of the number, so far as I know," continued the speaker, John C. McCoy, before the Old Settlers' Society of Jackson County, Missouri, "holds on to the chase, poor Tom Rule, who used to preach a pretty fair backwoods sermon, and boasted that with only hickory withes and a jackknife he could make a very good wagon, refused to be comforted or give up the chase after his beloved 'Far West.'

"Only last year I met him on Grand Avenue, mounted on a mountain mustang, his face, what little of it could be seen besides hair, looking very much like a small piece of buffalo meat, and with hair standing out like porcupine quills. He was spurring and belaboring his jaded mustang in an easterly direction, evidently, as I conjectured, bound to head off his favorite 'Far West' as it came round the world from sunrise . . ."

Poor Tom Rule was keeping faith with his phantom, an innocent, a "character," lost to the present by what failure in the past? We shall never know, but his enacted testimony to the power of what men shared and felt together so long before his cranky apparition in the streets of Kansas City in 1870 has in it a lingering eloquence, along with its pathos and absurdity. It was enough to move old Mr McCoy himself, in his conjecture, to a kind of national lyricism, a style of frontier poetry, in which spoke again the spirit which was codified for all in the Constitution itself: a new dawn was the metaphor. (When the sun rose over him as he returned from a nocturnal hunt, Davy Crockett lighted his pipe from it and walked on home, "introducin' people to the fresh daylight with a piece of sunrise in my pocket.")

Freedom remained the goal, of both nation and citizen; and the imperative appeal of Far West contained promise of freedom. Beyond material inducement and profession of motive, the Great West of Tom Rule and his comrades was an idea, a concept that stirred men, though perhaps at the time they could not have said how or why. But in irresistible response, they felt that source of energy which in the early years of the nineteenth century awakened the nation to awareness of its frontier westward, and to belief in it as the dimension of the American future. Some, like poor Tom Rule, in a sense came under the spell of the Western idea, lost in romance. Others, concerned with the immense American fact and all its operative details, brought Far West into the scheme of life and organized it in accord with the society of the United States.

The earliest venturers discovered Far West with their physical toil and endurance, and for the most part could then only talk of the experience within the frame of their separate lives. For those who would follow them in great numbers, information was needed.

The gold finds in California produced overland guidebooks in quantity, after 1849, to meet the wants of the fortune seekers who "rushed." But well before then, the experiences and places of the prairie voyage were brought to the public in a reasoned, precise, comprehensive account by a mid-American uniquely qualified by temperament and learning to describe the new lands.

He was Josiah Gregg, born in 1806. His father was a wheelwright who moved—"traipsed," as they said then—from Tennessee to Illinois, then to Missouri, where he settled his family near Cooper's Fort, close enough to the unmarked frontier for the Greggs to endure an Indian raid at Christmastime in 1814.

Necessarily it was a self-contained world into which Josiah Gregg was born, and he met all the varieties of his experience with the fortitude, ingenuity, and simple endurance common to the frontier character. But to these traits were added others which made him an uncommon man in his time and place, for he was more a man of mind than of muscle. In his childhood he was for the most part his own teacher, encouraged by his mother—an intelligent woman who saw in her son a special inclination for affairs of the intellect. (They said she could read diamond type without the aid of glasses at the age of seventy-seven.) As he grew, he considered learned professions, settled upon the law, but soon lost interest in it. Yet his general direction was unwavering, and he made his way through other studies —surveying, mathematics, elegant literature—and since there was no school he set one up and taught in it for a year.

At twenty-three he began to decline in health, from causes which his family, even the country doctor, could not determine. He seemed destined for an early death. With no certainty of success, the doctor on the edge of Far West gave what seemed a strange order in view of the invalid's extreme debility.

Since 1824 wagons for Santa Fe, over what came to be known as the Santa Fe Trail, were carrying on trade with Mexico in gradually increasing volume. The traders—some from St. Louis, others from their little frontier settlements—converged on Independence, Missouri, and when the train was complete, set out in their long lines of sunbonneted wagons over the unbounded prairies. It was a compelling, new American experience. It took everything men could give it in the way of attunement to wilderness.

Under the doctor's orders, the helpless Josiah, who could not even sit a horse, was placed lying down on a wagon bed and sent off to the prairies with a train. It was a risk, one which the doctor took with a profound intuition of the young man's need and nature. The strongest experience of the time, with its mysteries of change, discovery, and challenge, might well in its corporate energy call the invalid back to life, since nothing at home seemed to do so.

The prescription succeeded. Young Josiah recovered strength by the day. For a week he lay in the wagon; then he got up and was able to saddle his horse; soon he was riding a part of each day on the trail; and before much longer he was well enough to carry his share of the trailsman's duties. More, knowing he was on the way to a Mexican city, he studied Spanish, and by the time he reached there he could get along with the New Mexicans in their own language. He not only recovered—he found his vocation through his robustly curative regimen.

For it was life on the trail which brought his energies alive again—gave his eye and his mind new exercises in recording with the growing sense of duty of the born naturalist all aspects which he could observe of a great sweep of life new to him and, in fact, to the United States at large. Every evening, as he traveled, he recorded his observations in the little pocket notebooks with their wallet covers which he took along with him on that first journey, and on all subsequent ones.

Between 1831 and 1840 he made eight trips in all across the prairies and return, spending weeks or months at a time in Santa Fe. He prospered modestly in a business way as a trader. But his real profit lay in the notebooks, for they contained the raw material of facts from which he fashioned a book, *Commerce of the Prairies*, the first systematic and comprehensive description of the prairie culture and the Mexican society at the point where the trade turned southward from Santa Fe and led to its terminus at the city of Chihuahua. Natural science, human nature, and the life of freedom from formal society were the materials of his observations. His book was published in 1844. It became the monument to his life, and a guide to other travelers who took to Far West with the benefit of his information. The work had four editions in six years. It was the only book he published.

But in his diaries, which he kept as long as he was able, he left a further record of the brief rest of his life. He studied medicine in Kentucky and took a degree, but did not practice until he settled for a while in Saltillo, Mexico, remaining there after detaching himself from United States troops with whom he traveled as a guide and interpreter in the Mexican campaigns of 1846 and 1847. In Saltillo he served the people as a working physician until he heard the California news of 1849.

He then returned to the United States and with a small party set out to find a new trail overland to northern California and the commerce of the gold fields. There, having nearly reached his goal, he met his end at the age of forty-four, exhausted by hardship, the brutish scorn of his less enlightened companions, and his own character, which, with all its refinements of mind and taste, had a shrill and unbending aspect that made him candidly intolerant of society anywhere, and therefore its victim.

But he survives in his work, and we can see him in a fine 1844 daguerreotype: his sparely modeled face, fine, shadowed blue eye, frank cheekbones, good straight nose, well-chiseled mouth, and tapering chin. His thick dark hair is swept off his high forehead and is brushed loosely over his ears. It is a sensitive face, yet with a set to its jaw. Always a man of propriety, he dressed for his formal photograph, wearing a white shirt with a heavy black satin bow tie and a coat of stout broadcloth. He is in the conventional period uniform of polite society; but always he is uncomfortable there: would rather be out of it, standing almost six feet tall, dressed in a long homespun duster over a heavy linsey shirt, bulky trousers, and thick knee boots, and wearing a round, flat, wide-brimmed hat from which he could peer out of shade into the light of far distance, alert to all that is new ahead, ready to overtake it with a passion for fact, and a little something of poor Tom Rule's lost romance.

I

TO THE PRAIRIES

A VERY FAITH

IN 1812, IN HOWARD COUNTY, MISSOURI, ON
the Indian Frontier, there was a little United States community medieval in self-sufficiency and commonness of task. It
was Cooper's Fort. Set in a clearing, with farms around its
cluster of log buildings, a forest beyond, a well-worn road strag-
gling in generally from the east, and a few paths beginning off
toward the west, such a place was a little concentration of energy
typical of its time. It was a tiny pinpoint on a map labeled Far
West, a map that lived in people's thoughts, calling them like
the promise of all lands they ever dreamed about.

Far West was a very faith; steamboats and even children, according to the custom, were named for it; promises were
redeemed by it—a man to himself, a debtor to his neighbor, a
lover to his bride. It had the grand commonness of all hopes.

To Cooper's Fort, and other outposts like it, families came
from "back East." In 1812, a wheelwright named Harmon
Gregg brought his wife and children and joined the community
there, whose members first of all served each other in protection
from the two great hostilities that faced them: first, that of the
wilderness earth; second, that of the dispossessed Indians. Ready
and willing to find themselves good lives out of the land, the
settlers were forced to bundle together in stockades for safety.

What remains of the frontier achievements yields plenty of evidence that it was a triumph in what might be called earth relations, if not, with the Indian in mind, a triumph in human relations. Hard work in the ground and a vigilant eye on the distance—these might be the remembered preoccupations of a child who grew up there, where the road from the East ended, and the paths, like predictions, ventured westward through the woods and sought sight of the prairies, that great sea whose waves of rumor broke upon the shore of the American imagination in the nineteenth century.

In the week of Christmas, in 1814, the families at Cooper's Fort discovered directly what the term "Indian Frontier" meant.

The Harmon Greggs' youngest boy, Josiah, was eight years old. He never forgot the Indians coming—how they killed his Uncle William and stole his cousin, the young girl Patsy Gregg, and carried her off from the Fort. Sound of guns, sight of fire; listening in the woods where the air wandered high in the trees; the cold weather of Christmas; baffled pity for a girl as victim—such memories became character. The Indians were chased, the girl was recovered, and Christmas had its points after all. Even the most matter-of-fact boy would know excitement and be oddly sobered by such happenings. Josiah had seen much country already, in his eight years.

He came of a family of movers. His father was born in Kentucky and moved to North Carolina, and again to Tennessee, and again to Illinois, married to a woman from Pennsylvania. Getting on farther west was the most natural thing in the world to an able wife in those days. They stayed, finally, in Missouri. Of their several children, Josiah inherited most of the urge to keep on moving that his father and mother had shared with the people of their time and destiny.

New country! Far West!

Some of them had it in their blood.

BORDER BOY

To be in harmony with the border life, a man had first of all to be strong and ingenious physically. The jobs that had to be done were those of muscle—building, farming, killing and curing game. Harmon Gregg, abandoning his wheelwright's trade, became a farmer after he settled in the West. He taught his sons how to use tools, for this was the most useful thing they could know. Beyond that, he always said he wanted them to have the best education, probably meaning by it the very things to know which were pretty useless in pushing back the wilderness. But one of his boys was by nature predisposed toward such matters, and it was Josiah.

As a child he was delicate and was never asked to do the heavy labor of the farm and family. He was a calm, sweet-natured child, rather grave in his outlook, and as observant as an Indian. He read everything he could find in print, and thought much about what he read, and saw, and heard. "Myself cradled and educated upon the Indian border," he later said in a quaintly beautiful expression that sounds like Whitman, in speaking of his early days. He spoke of his father and mother as "such excellent parents." He liked to say that his education "had been received in the woods in a round log cabin." In his sick spells he was often dosed with "bitters," a forest curative made of whiskey mixed with black snakeroot, sarsaparilla roots, dock roots, dogwood and wild cherry barks, and gum of black pine. He was probably much alone, as a youngster. Solitude is a habit of the mind. It could well be born of the silences of the forest, if they were all over the memory of a childhood.

For four years the Greggs lived in Cooper's Fort and then settled a farm of their own. The ex-wheelwright, "excellent parent," found it difficult to educate his children—"a thing much desired by him." One of the Greggs wrote years later, "For some years teachers of ability were not in the Country, and the new settlers showed little inclination to spend either money or time for the education of their children—not even in the erection of comfortable school houses."

But there was a school of sorts, and Josiah was a leading scholar. His brother said that the other pupils used to apply to him for help in their studies of arithmetic as often as to the teacher. Josiah had a mathematical cast of mind, anyway—analytical, logical, consequent. If he was an infant pundit, he was also, in a sense, among the users of the frontier and the doers of physical jobs, the future. His effect was always to be intellectual. Quite possibly he was a fondly held misfit, the sickly boy with his head full of thoughts and patterns, in that society which was busy only with the tasks of survival.

One of the family could remember, long after, the days when spinning wheels and looms occupied almost the entire attention of the women. They made all the clothing, and the first thing a man did was to get him a wife, "so as to have her make his clothes."

On a Sabbath, they all went to church. The meetings were held at the cabins or in the groves, at the sign of the weather. The youngsters carried their shoes and stockings in their hands until within a short distance of the meeting house, then sat down and put them on. The first school was a pole cabin with a dirt floor covered with boards put on with weight poles, there being no nails to nail them with. People needed little money, since there were no unreasonable taxes. There was plenty of deer, turkey, and other game; plenty of wild honey. There were a great many wolves and snakes. At times there were many Indians passing through the country, hunting and camping.

It was a busy, intimate life.

But it was only a station on the way.

FRONTIER SCHOLAR

What is rumor but a temporary answer to an urgent question?

What lay farther west?

A few men had gone on and had returned with reports which often lost the truth as they circulated. One such man, the first one, was already a creature of legend. Alone, his direct influence, his example, and his path extended from North Carolina across the Mississippi. He was the genius of the wilderness, from whom it seemed to hold no secrets, and before whom it interposed no obstacles. As most men need others about them to complete their lives, to complete his he needed all the unsettled land he could find. As the nature of some men needs for fulfillment the creation of new theory, so his needed to behold new country. He was Daniel Boone, and it was by Boone's Lick Road that people finally reached the Santa Fe Trail. Boone's tradition had become one of the grand forces of the border, a part of the collective curiosity and wisdom of the people. Who knows what part it might play in a boy's life there, coaxing into his foreknowledge the aptitudes he would later show? In Josiah's solemn and maybe priggish boyhood there were little episodes that dramatized in miniature much of the experience he was afterward to know full-size.

For example, he built himself a quadrant of wood when he was about twelve and set to using it at odd little trials, such as measuring the heights of trees. The other forest boys refused to believe that he could really measure heights with the contraption and would argue in defense of the only way you could be sure about—and that was to climb up and take a rope and *see* how high it was. But Josiah knew without leaving the ground, by sighting with his rickety doodad.

It was a kind of situation he was often to be in later on—the theorist among the materialists. But it was also practice with a sort of technique which could in after years help a man to navigate the prairies, where at first men voyaged by the rudest reckonings. A French Creole named Lalande had wandered as far as Santa Fe in 1804. In 1805, James Purcell had gone there with the advice and guidance of some Indians he met. Captain Zebulon Pike returned from his Santa Fe visit of 1807 with many remarkable reports. Santa Fe was the most remote provincial capital of New Spain. Traders were not especially welcome. In 1812 a party headed by one McKnight was arrested and jailed in Chihuahua for nine years.

But their stories of the potential trade interested others.

In 1821, an Ohioan named Glenn went to Santa Fe with a small party "in perfect safety," and so did Captain William Becknell, who went out with four companions. This last venturer organized a party in the following year which was the first to proceed over the prairies by a more direct route, avoiding the upper Arkansas country, and encountering in the wilderness such privations as the first decade of the Santa Fe trade was to make fairly common. The trains consisted of pack animals, and consequently the volume of trade was small. But several parties made successful trips. Mexico was now independent of Spain. Trade was welcome, under controls.

The next step was to use wagons in the overland haul; and in 1824, a company of traders, "about eighty in number, among whom were several gentlemen of intelligence from Missouri," went overland, taking twenty-five wheeled vehicles, with about $30,000 worth of goods. One of the "gentlemen of intelligence" was Jacob Gregg, Josiah's older brother.

The trade was launched.

At home, Josiah and his brother John had taken up the study of surveying, without a teacher. Josiah was sixteen. In their study they presently came to Gunter's Scale, which neither of them understood. A neighbor had offered to help them if they needed it, so Josiah went to ask him about Gunter's Scale. He returned with the neighbor's advice to forget it, since they would never need it. According to his brother, Josiah's "countenance was fallen," but John agreed with the neighbor. But Josiah retired with his ignorance and presently emerged with the problem solved by himself. He could harness mathematics. If vast uncharted lands lay at hand, they must be measured. Surveying belonged in the arts and crafts that would most immediately make good use and sense in the new country, crafts that an inintelligent boy would turn to naturally, perhaps.

When he was eighteen years old, presumably having bankrupted all the official resources of local education, Josiah went to Clay County, in the new country, near Liberty, and opened a school, where he taught for one year.

In the next autumn, 1825, his family moved from the Howard County settlement of Cooper's Fort to the Blue River country in Jackson County. Missouri had become a state in 1821. The Greggs took up a farm near what was to be the site of Independence, which was founded two years later, in 1827. The soil was rich under a hard earth crust. It took five to six yoke of cattle to break the prairie sod. Ox teams plowed for sowing. Crops came rich. The land was high and rolling, with much timber where the creeks ran, and along the Missouri River. Some of the river bluffs were three hundred feet high, and there were abundant limestone quarries. Springs of pure water flowed among the hills. The Greggs set up a log house of a story and a half, which was weatherboarded long after it was built. Harmon Gregg settled down there for good, in Blue township, four miles northeast of Independence. No more traipsing for the Greggs as a family.

Now it was possible for the trivia of civilization and order and ingenuity to catch up. An articulate old party remembered long afterward how he saw a very peculiar thing one day in Fayette, Howard County, Missouri, in 1829.

A merchant from Booneville was talking to a tall, red-haired young man in front of the hotel; he drew out two cigars and then "took from his pocket something, the like of which I had never before seen . . . rubbed it on the sole of his boot, and lo! there was combustion fire. —Previous to that our resource to produce fire was the flint and steel, the punk and tinder."

A different, but equally symbolic, symptom of the new order of living was a census. Jacob Gregg took a census of Jackson County in 1826, when he was twenty-four years old, occupying ten days at the job, for ten dollars. Two years later, Jacob was a deputy sheriff of the county. This has the air of an intelligent family doing its part—not for any political advantage, because there was none; not spectacular, but useful.

As for how they lived, in the story-and-a-half log house, somebody remembered later that things were tucked "behind the glass in the parlor." It is a small enough bone by which to reconstruct a social skeleton; but by its reference to idle habit and family propriety, it somehow makes a ghost of a life.

UNCERTAIN YOUTH

When the problem of what to make of himself pressed upon Josiah, everybody agreed that his rather high-toned talents should find their order in some profession. So, "as well as from inclination, as the advice of friends," he agreed, and settled upon becoming a man of medicine. He applied to Dr John Sappington, of Saline County, Missouri, to take him as apprentice and student. This was the medical man who first preached widely the use of quinine in treatment of fever, and who wrote the first medical treatise west of the Mississippi (1844). He would have appealed to Josiah as a preceptor; but for reasons which we do not know, the doctor declined. Josiah then turned to the law, and read with diligence, but without enthusiasm. He said to his brother John that "law was the only study he had ever undertaken, in which he did not think he had been able to make reasonable progress." He said, "The Common Law may have been adapted to the age in which it originated; but it is a reproach to any people professing the civilization & equality of rights we do."

But he must have seemed plausible, at least, in his legal interim, because on the evening of the twenty-fourth of June 1829 he received a letter from a committee of eminent men of Jonesborough, asking him to "deliver an appropriate address" on the approaching Fourth of July. He was twenty-three years old, and it was a solemn honor to come to him. He wrote a letter in reply which is the first extended utterance of his to be saved. It is literate and elegant, with all the ceremonious ingenuity of its period. Our author must have been reading Johnson and Gibbon and harking to precepts in such matters as modesty and deference. He is honored by the invitation, but must protest that there are others far better suited to the—but we had better read the whole thing, as he wrote it:

Mount-Prairie, June 25, 1829.

GENTLEMEN:

Your polite note of yesterday,—informing me of your design to celebrate the Anniversary of our Independence, on the 4th. prox. at Jonesborough, and requesting me to deliver an appropriate address on the occasion,—was received last evening. It is, Gentlemen, with sentiments of emotion, that I acknowledge the respect shown me, in thus requesting me to become the "Speaker of the Day;" and I should be "thrice happy," did I think myself, in any degree, adequate to the task: But I fear—aye, I know—that those of you with whom I have had the honour of an acquaintance have greatly over-rated—and those with whom I have not, have been misinformed of, my talents and acquirements—else you would never have selected *me* to deliver *your* sentiments to an enlightened audience; when there are so many others of your fellow-citizens, who could (and, I presume, would) discharge the functions of the orator, infinitely more to the satisfaction of, not only to yourselves, but the contemplated auditory.

Yes, Gentlemen, were I ever so competent—and, what is more (with regard to my compliance), were I ever so self-conceited—I should feel an extreme diffidence in undertaking the performance of such a task, at this *late hour*,—engaged as I am in a business which occupies nearly all my time; and which it would neither be my interest, nor I presume, the will of my employers, for me to dismiss. Moreover, I have never delivered an address on such an occasion, nor do I make the least pretensions to oratory of any description. Therefore, I trust you will select some one else, whose leisure and talents may enable him to acquit himself with more honour than I should have it in my power to do. In the mean time, I will prepare such an address as my business may permit me to compose; which, should you fail (the time being short) in procuring another speaker, I will endeavour to deliver. It would be a very great gratification to me to be excused, for the reasons above, even after having written it—I shall not consider the time occupied idly spent.

I will endeavour to be at Jonesborough next Saturday, when we can make some further arrangements; yet, should I not, you may be assured, Gentlemen, that nothing which you may conceive would be conducive, in the slightest degree, to the enjoyment of yourselves and the company, will be too arduous to be attempted (though I fear not consummated) by one, who would be happy to be styled

Your Friend, and
Most ob't. Servant,

Josiah Gregg
(*Flourish*)

Messrs. G. E. Boswell
S. Martin
W. Prunty

A. Pearson
E. D. Sappington
B. E. Cooper

P.S. You did not mention, or even intimate, in your note, that there was any other person in contemplation, to be my co-adjutor. I should be very glad, should I eventually have to deliver an address, that I could have a "fellow-labourer," as mine must needs be short. Mr. P. W. Nawlin—or probably others with whom I am unacquainted—would, I have no doubt, deliver an address on the occasion.

J. Gregg.

How admirable this must have seemed to the addressees! What seemliness; what rich rhetorical confection; how adroit with dashes, how nimble those retreats into parenthesis, how placid the progress of a ninety-word sentence! And then, too, how tasteful, to refuse out of modesty, and in the next long breath, how considerate to go right ahead and accept the invitation; what good manners to preserve, until the postscript, even, the assumption that at the last minute a more suitable candidate will turn up, and of course carry off the honors of the day. Here, they must have thought, is a young man who will go far in his chosen field of endeavor, for in him all the virtues of the time appear to meet.

But while we smile at the manner, let us not forget the meaning of this letter, and of the address which it actually brought forth. He went and gave his speech, which was printed in the newspaper with favorable comment. The whole thing means that to Josiah Gregg and his six worthies of Jonesborough political independence and pride in its achievement were very real things and ought to be celebrated every July 4th, and not lightly. Therefore, he went to work and wrote a long speech, organized with a certain grandeur that alludes between the lines to the profitable study of the great British stylists of the eighteenth century, making several points that undoubtedly reflect his sincere passion for freedom and reverence for the American ideal.

All this bears direct evidence of the breadth of his education, which was begun, classically enough, in a log cabin. To those who need knowledge with a kind of hunger, there is passion in the very idea of an education. Knowledge is to be wrested from the most difficult circumstances and loved for its own sake.

As for what to do with himself, if the law was not going to satisfy him, what was open to Josiah? Schoolmaster? Man of science? These both would seem appropriate for him. And yet —and yet the strongest interest of his time and place was the transient life of the prairies—to become a mariner of the inland ocean. Men of action always responded to the typical creative experience, the new contribution, of their times. The values that were effectual on the frontier were first of all physical. In these, Josiah Gregg was deficient as a young man, after a delicate childhood.

He struggled with the law until 1830, and then his health broke down. His doctor and his friends advised him to give up the law. It was a losing fight anyway, as his remark to his brother had made plain. He went to visit some friends in the southern part of the state, and there, in September, he was really ill, apparently bedridden until the following spring, much "reduced and debilitated." He was so feeble he could not mount a horse. His illness was spoken of as a consumption; what brought it on him has never been clearly established. His doctor must have been a man of sympathy and discernment. When his patient was so weak that the ordinary daily acts and movements were all but beyond him, the doctor made up his mind and issued orders which must at first have sounded fantastic. He told Josiah to take a trip on the prairies with a train going to Santa Fe. It would mean the hardest kind of travel. There was barely a road. The wagons were comfortless. Hardy men rode their horses all day, and some even walked. What reason was there to suppose that a dying youth would survive such a venture?

Perhaps the doctor concluded that the young man's illness was every bit as environmental as it was physical. The fact is that Josiah was put into a prairie wagon, and started off, and began to mend at once.

By act of Congress in 1825, authority was given to "the president of the United States to cause a road to be marked out from the western frontier of Missouri to the confines of New Mexico." For $1,000 in money payment, and $600 in merchandise, the United States government got the right of way for the Santa Fe Trail from the Osage and Kansa Indians. The organized trade began successively at the eastern terminal of Old Franklin, Independence, Westport, and then Westport Landing (Kansas City). Before 1824 the traders used pack mules, and a train consisted of from ten to one hundred and fifty pack animals. Usually one man had charge of five or six pack horses, though sometimes as many as fifteen. They could travel from fifteen to thirty miles a day. When the wagons were introduced in 1824, they found a route of eight hundred miles which was more easily traversed by wheeled vehicles than any other trail of like distance in the United States.

Small companies of traders could come and go without fear of the Indians, when the trade began. But (again) it is bitterly agreed by men who had been there that the white man cheated and often killed in cold blood even a friendly Indian who came intending good rather than harm. Of the several ventures successfully made before 1825, Josiah wrote to his brother John, ". . . up to the time you returned [from a New Mexican trading trip] no one had been killed, I believe." If the earlier traders could make their voyages in peace, the later ones could have. Indians became a hazard only as the traders grew confident.

When he first set out in the caravan, Josiah had to travel altogether in the light wagon. They were headed for Santa Fe, the

Mexican outpost; so day after day, lying on the wagon bed
under the sunny wagon sheets, he pursued not only his health
but also the Spanish language. By the time he got there, he had
a secure hold on the rudiments of both. Though unable to
mount a horse when they sent him out on the prairies on the
light wagon, within the first week of prairie travel he saddled
his own pony, and rode part of each day; "and when we reached
the buffalo range, I was not only as eager for the chase as the
sturdiest of my companions, but I enjoyed far more exquisitely
my share of the buffalo meat" than all the finicking "supply of
such commodities" as he had deemed essential to his comfort
and health.

Indeed, ever after, he was completely well only when he was
on the plains—moving about, observing, facing toil and hazard;
and ever after, on his return home, he was sick, "rabid," morose,
restless. With his delicate physique he entered upon a life which
required genuine robustness in most others. Perhaps what is
nowadays called "compensation" in behavior—with a rather
superior air—is often more than just that; perhaps it is an or-
ganically curative effort of life to seek a proper balance by over-
coming deficiencies.

Anyway, he went and, within the modest measure of one man,
acted in harmony with the keynote, the typical function, of the
nation in the nineteenth century. These were the most significant
ten weeks of his lifetime, these first weeks on the plains, for they
gave him strength and presented him daily with new aspects of
a life, an experience, a culture, to which he devoted years of
observation and thought; becoming, in the process, one of the
primal contributors to our record of the American grain, upon
which is founded our literature of experience, that broad base of
our culture upon which in turn will be erected the future likeness of our national imagination.

John Gregg wrote of his brother Josiah that "it had been his
habit from early youth to note down everything he deemed

worthy of remembrance. This habit had been well preserved in during the time he was engaged in the Santa Fe trade, but without the intention at the time of making any other use of it more than a mere book of reference to strengthen his own memory."

THE PLAINSMAN

With the recovery of his health, Josiah entered actively upon the life of a trader, serving first as bookkeeper to the owner of "an enterprise," as the prairie ventures were called, and later as master of his own. He did reasonably well in a business way, though he was never a rich man.

His activities on these ventures were twofold. On the one hand, he was a shrewd man of business, estimating his Mexican markets with pretty fair judgment, and buying goods carefully, freighting them across the grassy ocean through chancy conditions; setting up his shop in Santa Fe and holding sales during the winters; learning how to conquer the plains by experience, and exchanging his experiences with other traders until a way of commerce was built up; conducting his affairs with the strictest decorum and honesty, which earned him respect. On the other hand, he was hard to pin down with a label, because his interests and offices were so varied and so far removed from the motives of trade. In his second character as a plainsman, Gregg was a scientist, a writer, an encyclopedist of a New World; and he never took a trading trip that did not also serve him—in a sort of extension of Yankee cleverness—as a scientific expedition, for he kept notes and diaries and took observations and recorded phenomena, and collected lore, and scratched the truth out of rumor and legend, and managed to pursue the intellectual life alongside the commercial, with success in both.

There was much to study; there were many rewards for sober

curiosity. Once business matters had been intelligently dealt with, there were all the oddnesses—the differences—in a foreign country to be noted. And the life of the prairies! How could any man with a quick mind fail to see its amazing dimensions, its amplitude for the spirit, its triumphs of ingenuity among the men who met brand-new conditions every day and solved them in terms necessarily new also?

In all, Gregg spent nine years as a Santa Fe trader, in his eight trips, four out and four back. He was in a position to know much about "the origin and progressive development of the Santa Fe trade." The life of the traders' camp was his own, and the discipline of men crossing the grand plains was his code. The history, the resources, the customs, the government, the Indian heritage of northern Mexico had never been reported upon with any degree of fullness. For that matter, the animals and aborigines of the plains were new subjects in the 1830s. All these things interested him tremendously. He carried a field desk with him, and ink, and paper bound into little pocketbooks, pens, a few instruments, some books. These possessions were like the little links of a broken chain that signified freedom to him. If a man had these things, what on earth else did he need? Owning other things, immovable things, tied you down . . .

If you recorded a fact exactly enough, it was astonishing how satisfying that could be.

Thus, in the pursuit of truth, the reward was simply the truth for its own sake.

So he wrote every day in his diary. It is a record in which objective experience is the hero. During his nine years on the plains, he filled notebook after notebook, and when he set it down that he left Santa Fe on the twenty-fifth of February in 1840, marking the end of his "enterprises," the great experience of his life was over, and the prairies were behind him.

What they had meant to him!

"Since that time," he wrote later, "I have striven in vain to reconcile myself to the even tenor of civilized life in the United States; and have sought in its amusements and in society a substitute for those high excitements which have attached me so strongly to prairie life. . . . Scarcely a day passes without my experiencing a pang of regret that I am not now roving at large upon those western plains. Nor do I find my taste peculiar; for I have hardly known a man, who has ever become familiar with the kind of life which I have led for so many years, that has not relinquished it with regret.

"There is more than one way of explaining this apparent incongruity. In the first place—the wild, unsettled and independent life of the Prairie trader, makes perfect freedom from nearly every kind of social dependence an absolute necessity of his being. He is in daily, nay, hourly exposure of his life and property, and in the habit of relying upon his own arm and his own gun for both protection and support. Is he wronged? No court or jury is called to adjudicate upon his disputes or his abuses, save his own conscience; and no powers are invoked to redress them, save those with which the God of Nature has endowed him. He knows no government—no laws, save those of his own creation and adoption. He lives in no society which he must look up to or propitiate. The exchange of this untrammelled condition—this sovereign independence, for a life in civilization, where both his physical and moral freedom are invaded at every turn, is certainly likely to commend itself to but few,—not even to all those who have been educated to find their enjoyments in the arts and elegancies peculiar to civilized society . . .

"A 'tour on the Prairies' is certainly a *dangerous* experiment for him who would live a quiet contented life at home among his friends and relatives; not so dangerous to life or health, as prejudicial to his domestic habits . . .

"There is another consideration which, with most men of the Prairies, operates seriously against their reconciliation to the habits of civilized life. . . . A long absence from such society generally obliterates from their minds most of the common laws of social intercourse, which are so necessary to a man of the world . . .

"It will hardly be a matter of surprise then, when I add, that this passion for Prairie life, how paradoxical soever it may seem will be very apt to lead me upon the Plains again, to spread my bed with the mustang and the buffalo, under the broad canopy of heaven,—there to seek to maintain undisturbed my confidence in men, by fraternizing with the little prairie dogs and wild colts, and the still wilder Indians—the *unconquered Sabaeans* of the Great American Deserts."

In spite of its period clichés, this apologia for the prairie life is a poem in itself and a striking, wide-open view into his very heart and character. Here are suggested his views of his time, of society; his scholarly misanthropy; the flavor of his thought, and the rhythm of it. The longing it expressed was never to be gratified again. The uneasiness it confesses about a return to "civilized life" was to send him forth in various fields and travels, in all of which his destiny—that is, his character of inquirer and recorder—was furthered. This hymn to the land which matured him and gave him his health and caused him to share directly in the arch-typical experience of his time, the pursuit of Far West, is one man's apprehension of the emotion, unacknowledged, unorganized, unanimous, that made our national character what it was then; and even today, those words have in them some indescribable nostalgia, the tug of natural desire, and the trouble, and the gratefulness, of its fulfillment.

ALIEN AT HOME

After he left the prairies forever, in 1840, Josiah remained a little over a year in Jackson County, Missouri, with his parents. He could never stay home for long after that roving existence. Indeed, he was never again at home in the social climate of the United States. American standards, customs, the things that were expected of polite young gentlemen in the way of success— all seemed alien to him and irked him in obscure fashion. Sometimes he sounds, in his little scribbled notes, almost in despair at himself for needing a more lonesome society than the average. Though propriety has always been the enemy of curiosity, he was both the most proper and most curious of men, and it was not long before he was on the move once more.

In June 1841, he records that he "resolved to take a trip into Texas, for the purpose of looking at the country," a venture "partly on business and partly to see the country." These could stand as mottoes for his motives over his whole life. He went to the neighboring republic to buy and sell mules, and picked up a good trade, and bought some land. Along his whole route he recorded the condition of the country. We may know a good deal about the Texas nation by reading his notes—the topography of the land; the soil's composition; the quality of the water; the nature of the people, the kinds of trees, and the states of health dictated by the terrain; evidences of sloth or cleverness in the population; and in at least once instance he gives us a vigorous blast at the politics of Texas, when he witnessed the second inauguration of General Houston as president and decided that he was an ungallant, overrated, frontier show-off. All these particulars are set forth with confidence derived from his larger view of life, so that again we are constantly glimpsing Gregg himself through the shapely proportions of his observations and arguments.

He returned home again after the Texas trip and evidently gave himself up to meditation and odd jobs, including a new survey of the town of Van Buren, Arkansas (where John Gregg now lived), for which he was to receive $900 "Arkansas money." Further commercial ventures were also in the wind, in partnership with his brother John and George C. Pickett, with whom he sustained relations all his life. But it was the meditative knack which was to prove most interesting to him and all of us, for, he recorded in his diary on January 1, 1843, "it was a little prior to this time that I commenced preparing notes for the compilation of a work on 'Santa Fe and the Prairies.' I now supposed I would be able to publish it during the following summer."

It was a memorable winter, what with earthquakes, a comet, extraordinary cold, flood. He watched—and recorded—these phenomena, and his literary materials took shape. In July he went East to see about finishing the manuscript and finding a publisher.

In Philadelphia he was unable to work because of the noises in the street; so he went to board in Camden, New Jersey, at $4 a week. He wrote to his brother that after an attack of influenza, which was epidemic in Philadelphia that year, he had a very severe pain in the head ("bordering on inflammation of the brain"). A physician told him it was "in the ramification of the nostril, and not in the brain." But his hair "commenced shedding as fast as a horse in the spring," so he shaved his head and began to wear a toupee until the natural growth should come out long enough. The pain, he indicates, is what accounts for a sharp letter he had written home last time, evidently full of critical reflections upon his relatives-in-law, and upon Pickett, the partner.

"I think I said something about the aristocratical notions of

Mrs. McClellan and some of the family. I don't hold any of them to blame; for it is the consequences of education. We were educated in the sheerest democracy, which I deem a great fortune, and consequently would entertain different notions . . . But whosoever would in the least ill-treat my parents, would elicit angry observations from me . . ."

Do we read, between these lines, the evidences of one of those farces of snobbery which American society so often witnesses? It sounds as though Mrs McClellan, mother-in-law of the Gregg daughter, had been "aristocratical" with Mrs Gregg, the mother democrat, and had been censured very sharply by Josiah. It is a pleasure to think so; for a man who had claimed as his own the natural laws of prairie life would see and hate whatever highfalutin' nonsense might have crept into Western social life as the frontier receded.

He is troubled by something else, too. Pickett, the elder partner, had been free with advice, whose kind intentions are freely acknowledged, but: "I only felt mortified that he should have seemed to conclude it necessary to take me 'under guardianship'—giving indications sometimes that he thought me hardly capable of taking care of myself." It was too bad that even his friends at home did not understand him. But what else might they see in him but an "impractical" and rather eccentric sort, scratching around the ground for bits of mineral to look at, speculating upon the philosophies of things so familiar that everybody else took them for granted, and wearing a yardstick for a spine, and ethics like a sniff?

THE BOOK

"Nothing could induce me to embark in a United States business," he wrote to John, from Philadelphia, where he was working hard at writing. He said that if he had known how difficult
it was going to be, he would probably never have undertaken
the job of writing the book; but having begun it, he behaved
professionally and finished it, bit by bit: "My motto is 'Go
ahead.'" Naturally, he is wondering about publishers and has
been "strongly recommended to the Harpers; and they are
perhaps the most popular publishers in the U.S." But like many
a first book, his was to go the rounds. He wrote down an impression of a new acquaintance in Philadelphia, one Griggs,
whose enthusiasm was hardly welcome, and who rushed the
author into an introduction to the Philadelphia publishers Carey
and Hart, though he much preferred to wait and see what could
be arranged in New York; whereupon the new friend made the
further mistake of writing Harpers a pretty strong letter, and
in general making Gregg suspicious "by that behavior typical of
the fringe citizens of the world of arts and letters who sometimes seem more officious than generous." Gregg finally decided
that his champion was "horribly double-faced."

Meanwhile, he was attending to details of a business nature
for the trading firm organized by his brother and Mr Pickett,
with himself. He saw merchants and dealers and visited the
house of Derringer to buy pistols (presumably in quantity, for
trade), and took none because he found none good enough. He
moved his quarters several times; if it was not the noise, it was
the bother of ferrying across from Camden. Work on the book
continued, until he was ready to go to New York with the manuscript. Harpers took some of it to look at, but were busy and

could not report until the next week. "My confidence has sunk as the 'crisis' approaches—I now feel more doubtful than ever" —this in December of 1843. But he shopped around elsewhere, and in a few weeks a contract had been signed with Messrs D. Appleton & Co. Perhaps it was they who suggested that he get professional help in preparing the book for publication. While under contract to Appleton's, Gregg engaged a helper.

This was a remarkable creature who called himself Count Louis Ferdinand Tasistro, who had played Hamlet in Philadelphia in 1831, and who eleven years later published a book entitled *Random Shots and Southern Breezes* (which sounds like a polka of the period). He was long employed at the State Department in Washington as a translator, and he appears to have been one of those romantics who elegantly impose their conception of life upon other persons' realities. We can see him, gulling our plainsman with hints of influence and the small grandeurs of the literary dandy. What we do know now is something of Gregg's temperament, and it is not long—a matter of a few weeks—until he has irascibly parted from the exquisite fraud, whose tendency was to rewrite Gregg's painstaking text until it presented, to the current romantic taste, a more flowery, if less factual, picture of the prairies. "Owing to the rascality and ill-temper of Tasistro, I withdrew my MS from him . . . and got the aid of one John Bigelow to assist me to finish revising or preparing my work for the press."

William Cullen Bryant had advised Gregg to seek out Bigelow, and he did, being introduced to him by one John W. Leavitt. A young member of the New York bar, Bigelow was later eminent as Bryant's co-editor on the New York *Evening Post* (1848). Later on, of course, he was known as a diplomatist, and as the author of many volumes in history. Though the *Dictionary of American Biography* gives no mention of his association with Gregg, he himself left a few notes which illuminate the part he played in working with Gregg on his book. He said

Gregg was "morbidly conscientious," and it is such a good esti-
mate that we believe him, too, when he says Tasistro had "no
such infirmity." Romantic oil and unsalty water—they would
never mix.

There have been various claims that Gregg's helpers—
Bigelow especially—ought to be regarded as his co-authors. But
Bigelow himself disposed of any but the most modest claims for
his part in the making of a book which, with prompt perception,
he declared to have "great and enduring value." He wrote,
"My laundry work added no more value to the washing of it
than the washing and ironing adds to the value of a new
garment."

At first, all looked well for the work in progress; but in
March 1844, the contract with Appleton was dissolved by mu-
tual agreement, and a new one arranged with Henry G.
Langley. The preparations were exhilarating. Bigelow was not
only a good workman but a friend. They planned outings together—the Catskills, West Point. What would the reviewers
say? In June, advance notices were appearing. One appeared in
the *Democratic Review*. Was the fact ever up to the enchanted
anticipation? That review for example: ". . . since I have had
time to read it, I find it not a very good one. The young man
who wrote it stands high as a literary character, and had examined my book thoroughly; so that I thought he could have
made a better selection than he did from it."

The critic was simply not intelligent enough—one of those
who in combing a book exhaustively can snare everything but
the point: this would be the author's conclusion, mourning his
work in memory of his intention.

But if a man was simply not bright enough, he could be forgiven. What was really reprehensible was a lazy critic, even another "gentleman of high repute"; a wretch who was "too lazy
to examine the book closely himself, and so made up his review
[in the *New York World*] from a copy of the *Democratic Re-*

view . . . so that the notice in the *New York World* is much
of the same tenor as that in the *Democratic*." When you recall
that the *original* review left something to be desired, this is a
heavy blow. Still, he sent it to John, now at Shreveport, a gauge
from the great world successfully challenged.—One thing about
authors is their conformity to type: "I have some hope of doing
fairly with my book." Another thing is their faith in publishers,
and the articles thereof: "One thing at least, the publishers will
make arrangements to have it sufficiently puffed."

Everything was finished at last, and on the last day of June
1844 he left for the West. "Mr. Langley expects to publish my
work in about ten days. Having got about 100 copies bound,
took them West with me. Work comprises two vols. 12mo, 320
and 318 pages. Title: 'Commerce of the Prairies: or Journal of
a Santa Fe Trader, during Eight Expeditions Across the Great
Western Plains and a Residence of Nearly Nine Years in Northern Mexico Illustrated with Maps and Engravings.' "

It was surely a satisfaction to be going home with his hundred
copies of that book which held so much of his life, typical of his
place and time.

It took him twenty-six days to go from New York to Shreveport, Louisiana, by rail, steamboat, and carriage. He went from
New York to Philadelphia to Pittsburgh by rail; and then by
steamer from Pittsburgh to Cincinnati to Louisville, which cost
five dollars. Late in the evening the steamer *Bunker Hill* left
Louisville for New Orleans, scheduled to stop at the mouth of
the Red River, to which point the fare was twelve dollars. But
after three days on the *Bunker Hill* he left her at Mills Point,
"on account of some insulting conduct of the officers, particularly
the clerk." He had a perpetual feud with pursers and clerks and
hotel keepers, and other purveyors to the public, at whose hands
he records time and again the suffering of insults, whose exact
nature is never stated, so that our only impression is one of dignity outraged, and we may be excused for speculating whether

it was the kind of dignity that positively glares an invitation to outrage. His fury at the clerk of the *Bunker Hill* cost him a lay-over, and at noon the next day he boarded the steamer *Talley-rand* and went on down the river with a less abrasive crew. On the twenty-sixth of July he was at his brother John's place, eight miles from Shreveport, "at 2 o'clock."

The book must have gone well during the summer. Bigelow, in New York, was a sort of agent and made himself felt on its behalf through reviews, contacts with the publishers, and so forth. By fall, a second edition was preparing; and a new pref-ace, some corrections in the type, and other interesting differ-ences were being readied. Gregg sustained a correspondence with Bigelow about all such matters of shop, and in the most friendly tone. (Indeed, only once in their exchange of letters, which went on for years, does Gregg address his friend with anything but warmth and respect; and then he was put out at not having re-ceived an answer to a couple of letters: ". . . nothing grinds me more than to have a friend refuse to answer a letter, especially as I stated I would not write again till I got an answer.")

He reports that during the current summer his father died; and that his own health, a little improved, was further bene-fited by a return to the prairies on a brief tour which had started out as a buffalo hunt but which, on the backing out of all the other members, turned into a bee hunt, with Gregg joining a party going out after wild honey. They found some, but not enough for commercial purposes, and returned disgruntled—all but Josiah, who had known again the scale on which daily existence was full of rewards of the simplest kind. When he came home again, he caught cold. He could not help contrasting this with the fact that on the plains, with the rudest exposures, he had not had even "the slightest catarrh."

There was no doubt about it—roots did not nourish him; they only tied him down. "My organ of inhabitiveness," he wrote (in the dreary elegance of the period science of phrenology), "is, I believe, entirely annihilated, and my desire to be on the 'wild roam' continues to increase." Perhaps a trip to Mexico? Would Bigelow go along? "Have you any idea of such a tramp? Should I engage in another expedition of the kind, nothing would gratify me more than to have you for a *compagnon de voyage*. I think we could pass some more agreeable hours than while pouring [*sic*] over musty law books or mustier manuscripts. But I hope to have the pleasure of seeing you and communicating with you *viva voce* in the course of the next month . . ."

For affairs of the second edition were taking him back to New York in November. He saw Bigelow, but nothing came of the scheme for a Mexican trip together. Corrections in the book were made, and Bigelow was useful again. It was a flying trip. By December he was on the way back to John Gregg's at Shreveport. There is a sense of another phase finished, a useful and important book safely established. One thing was clear, though: ". . . I have formed a resolution never to live south of Jackson Co., Missouri. No part of the climate can my constitution support except it be western Texas or Oregon; but my plans for the future are not fully laid."

II

AMERICAN FACTS

OBSERVATION
AND FEELING

THE IDEAL OR TYPICAL FORM TAKEN BY natural science in nineteenth-century America was description of frontiers. The great American fact of the time was not intellectual, like Darwin's theory in England and Huxley's preaching of it. It was geographical, the apprehension of a whole new world of creatures and places. All energies of the explorers and settlers of that world were turned, first, to knowing it well, and, second, to setting a wide knowledge of it. Pike did this; so did Audubon, and all the others, in the wake of those early Jesuits whose narratives gave first word of the great mid-continent area. Josiah Gregg's *Commerce of the Prairies* is a monument to that characteristic aspect of natural science in which America discovered herself during the momentous decades which marched from the Atlantic to the Pacific. In its pages lies the prairie culture; and because he reported so carefully what he saw, he gave us, too, a reflection of himself. When we listen to his account—his description of the land and the air, of the travelers of his company, of the Indians they encountered, of the Mexicans they found at the end of the trail—we are listening to what he thought, and did, and valued, until the whole becomes an apologia for a way of life to which he owed all the content that he ever knew, and which moves us as the truth always moves us when it is held sacred.

The 1844 edition published by Henry Langley of New York had a sturdy success, and went through five reprintings during the next ten years. An edition came out in England, and a German translation appeared in 1845. The reviewers were agreeable; scholars were attentive; but literary historians were, later, inattentive. Very little was known about the author—a modest, indeed an unsocial, man—until the discovery of his diaries and other manuscripts.* We know now that all his life Gregg kept careful "memoranda" (as he called them) of his observations and activities. In 1840 he left the prairies forever; but he had nine years' diaries with him, and out of them he fashioned, with high literary skill, the ablest account we have of the Westward adventure. Other accounts were possibly as accurate, and may have ranged further; but what other one has the sensitivity which turns observation into vision, and feeling into art?

THE LAND AND THE AIR

Gregg continually saw the prairie experience in terms of the ocean, the most immediate suggestion of its vastness and quality. "The grand prairie ocean," he wrote. "All is as level as the sea, and the compass was our surest, as well as principal guide." And "merchants conveying their goods across the prairies in wagons, should . . . be as much entitled to the protection of the Government, as those who transport them in vessels across the ocean." During the settlement of the Mexican boundary dispute,

---

* In the 1930s. See Editor's Introduction in Diary & Letters of Josiah Gregg, *Southwestern Enterprises, 1840–1847*, edited by Maurice Garland Fulton, with an introduction by Paul Horgan. Norman: University of Oklahoma Press, 1941. See also the preface in the present volume.

armies of both countries should "indiscriminately range upon this desert, as ships of war upon the ocean." And "a ledge of wave-like yellow sandy ridges and hillocks spreading far beyond" carried to his eye the metaphor of the sea.

His observations by-the-way tell us as much as anything could about the flavor of prairie nature. He speaks of the "bleakest rains and the hottest suns of these bare plains," and we know something as poetry would tell it to us, for the words somehow hold more than they say. The great clarity of light, the prairie sky, and the emanations of the earth interest him. He brings us an account of the optical illusions which travelers always wondered at, and which made a heap of buffalo bones "stretch upward to the height of several feet, so as to present the appearance of so many human beings. Ravens in the same way are not unfrequently taken for Indians, as well as for buffalo; and a herd of the latter upon a distant plain often appear so increased in bulk that they would be mistaken by the inexperienced for a grove of trees. This is usually attended with a continual waving and looming, which so often writhe and distort distant objects as to render them too indistinct to be discriminated." It is a marvel for later travelers to be warned of; indeed, the whole prairie is so new that everything must be explained. "The illusion" he has just described "seems to be occasioned by gaseous vapors rising from the ground while the beaming rays of the sun are darting upon it." The mirages, or "false ponds," which so often and so cruelly disappointed thirsting travelers, are explained in an economy of reason and word, thus: ". . . the opposite sky, being reflected in a *pond of gas,* gives the appearance of water."

Prairie culture takes in the sky, always. "We were encamped at noon, when a murky cloud issued from behind the mountains, and, after hovering over us for a few minutes, gave vent to one of those tremendous peals of thunder . . . making the elements tremble, and leaving us so stunned and confounded . . .

frightful thunder-gusts . . . I was deeply impressed." What is the curious flavor of intimacy in this? He has encompassed a vast act of nature as if he were a painter, able to command the elements in a little square of canvas. It is because he saw so singly and directly that he can do this, no matter what the scale of proportions. In finding trail and direction, what is an unexpected hazard? ". . . the innumerable buffalo paths, with which these plains are furrowed, and which are exceedingly perplexing to the bewildered prairie traveller. In a great many places which I have observed, they have all the appearance of immense highways, over which entire armies would seem to have frequently passed." The prairie scale is in that, too; and we see.

For he was unable to retail his experiences simply with a recital of facts. If he had stopped there, his book would be only another guidebook. Not that fact was ever unimportant. On the contrary, he loved it with a scientist's passion. But spirit, or implication, or flavor always attended his news, and gave it double sense. Toward the end of his book he speculates on the future, anticipates the prairie cities, and makes prophecy of the kind of effort government would be making a hundred years later to reclaim arid, eroded country:

The high plains seem too dry and lifeless to produce timber; yet might not the vicissitudes of nature operate a change likewise upon the seasons? Why may we not suppose that the genial influences of civilization—that extensive cultivation of the earth—might contribute to the multiplication of showers, as it certainly does of fountains? Or that the shady groves, as they advance on the prairies, may have some effect upon the seasons? . . . May we not hope that these sterile regions might yet be thus revived and fertilized, and their surface covered one day by flourishing settlements to the Rocky Mountains?

His phrase "genial influence of civilization" is the expression of a man who saw the natural chances of the earth and wanted

for them non-wasteful use by men. ("Genial" here means "conducive to growth"—a period touch.) The book was written in
the early forties, and is innocent of the idea, so very shortly to
become a political passion in America, of empire to the Pacific
Ocean. But in its spirit Gregg's book has the spaciousness of
the land he describes, and we will pass on to a few notes about the
men who made up the companies, and their ways of meeting
the daily obstacles to their progress, and their myths and their
morality.

THE TRAVELERS

Never was there a more diverse company of men. "It is seldom
that such a variety of ingredients are found mixed up in so small
a compass." There were men of seven distinct nations, and each
spoke his native language: a voluble and gesticulatory French-
man, and "two phlegmatic wanderers from Germany," and two
Polish exiles, wonderfully credited with "calm eccentricity," and
some Indians, and Mexicans, and the Americans—who "were
mostly backwoodsmen, who could handle the rifle far better than
the whip." "The wild and motley aspect of the caravan can be
but imperfectly conceived without an idea of the costumes of its
various members. The most 'fashionable' prairie dress is the
fustian frock of the city-bred merchant furnished with a multi-
tude of pockets capable of accommodating a variety of 'extra
tackling'; then there is the backwoodsman with his linsey or
leather hunting shirt—the farmer with his blue jean coat—the
wagoner with his flannel-sleeve vest . . ." These men carried
firearms in "also an equally interesting medley. The frontier
hunter sticks to his rifle . . . the sportsman from the interior
flourishes his double-barrelled fowling-piece . . . 'repeating'

arms have lately been brought into use upon the Prairies . . . A great many were furnished beside with a bountiful supply of pistols and knives of every description."

"The insatiable appetite, acquired by travellers upon the Prairies is almost incredible, and the quantity of coffee drunk is still more so. It is an unfailing and apparently indispensable beverage, served at every meal—even under the broiling noonday sun, the wagoner will rarely fail to replenish a second time, his huge tin cup."

Gregg later on speaks of the low mortality of the early journeys. It was a condition that tied up with the work the travelers were doing. Such affirmative experience and acts as theirs had health in them, and life, and regularity from simply a hygienic view. But beyond that, they believed in their work, and had a sense of need and worth. In the whole Westward trend there was somewhere a spirit of health. Gregg himself set out a sickling, and came alive of it.

It was a spirit exhibited in their observance of the Fourth of July on the prairies. Alone on the wide plains, they celebrated with guns, fifes and drums, and gave freedom to "that joy which plays around the heart of every American on the anniversary of this triumphant day." That was a sincere and exact description of a state of feeling. There was an immediate and unified feeling of relation to the United States idea then. They were all still close to what had been won for and by the Republic. They were making physical compacts with the extent and character of the land. They felt—whether they talked of it or not—that they were individually and vitally part of that land and its politics. It is a feeling which their heirs would have to discover in terms of the social challenges of a later time.

THE PRAIRIE SCALE

Josiah Gregg usually rode a mile or two ahead of the train. How active must observation and judgment be to find the trail where none showed! The trail was eventually made by passage of wheels during and after a season of rain in 1834, which left ruts. Until then, the voyagers navigated the prairie oceans as if anew each time. "Since yesterday afternoon," says an entry in the trail diary of Gregg, "we have been travelling over a country tolerably sandy, covered with tall coarse grass, but it is firm enough to afford a reasonable road."

And that is how roads got made. In a big train, there were four lines of march, and their ruts went parallel where they could. When Indians attacked, each of the four lines would maneuver and become a side to a "corral" of wagons, a wheeled fort.

There was a culture of streams, on the plains. "When caravans are able to cross in the evening, they seldom stop on the near side of a stream—first, because if it happens to rain during the night, it may become flooded, and cause both detention and trouble: again, though the stream be not impassable after rain, the banks become slippery and difficult to ascend. A third and still more important reason is, that, even supposing the contingency of rain does not occur, teams will rarely pull as well in 'cold collars,' as wagoners term it—that is, when fresh geared— as in the progress of the day's travel. When a heavy pull is just at hand in the morning, wagoners sometimes resort to the expedient"—and what a picture it makes, of some archaic grace in necessity—"the expedient of driving a circuit upon the Prairie, before venturing to 'take the bank.' "

Sometimes they had to take their wagons to pieces in order

to ford heavy streams. They could not possibly have prepared in advance for a need like that. To be wise on this day, according to its needs, seems to have been their unspoken philosophy, which required nothing of tomorrow. "The truth is, upon leaving one watering-place, we never knew where we would find the next."

Once, yesterday caught up with today in a dangerous manner. "Our fire was carelessly permitted to communicate with the prairie grass. As there was a head wind blowing at the time, we very soon got out of reach of the conflagration: but the next day, the wind having changed, the fire was again perceived in our rear approaching us at a very brisk pace." He says everybody who ventured in these trains experienced the danger from such fires, which he superbly calls "sweeping visitations." The party struck a "long trot," and presently reached a cove, or inlet, of shorter grass, where the great grassy ocean came to bottom, and the fire burned more slowly and stopped. How often he spoke of the sea when he meant the prairies.

Eleven to fifteen miles a day was evidently good progress. It took ten weeks to go out to Santa Fe with laden wagons.

The return trip Eastward, with empty wagons, lasted only forty days, and was commonly made as winter approached. They hastened to be home. The time consumed in "closing an enterprise" was often a year—the trip out, the merchandising of the stores, the building of future custom, the trip back. One enterprise which Gregg accompanied took home $150,000 in specie and bullion from "the previous year's adventure."

There is a little observation, a footnote to prairie culture, which Gregg makes upon a return home from a New Mexican journey. He says that he "had an opportunity of experiencing a delusion which had been the frequent subject of remark by travelers on the Prairies before. Accustomed as we had been for some months to our little mules, and the equally small-sized Mexican ponies, our sight became so adjusted to their proportions, that when we came to look upon the commonest hackney of our frontier horses, it appeared to be almost a monster. I have frequently heard exclamations of this kind from the new arrivals:—'How the Missourians have improved their breed of horses!'—'What a huge gelding!'—'Did you ever see such an animal!'"

It is these curious and unexpected details that reveal the observer and the man inclined to share his odd knowledge. And the moralist added, "This delusion is frequently availed of by the frontiersmen to put off their meanest horses to these deluded travellers for the most enormous prices."

In what Gregg calls the "Olympus of Prairie mythology" the exploits and legends of plainsmen were secured by conversation. The source of both myths and morals was the way men braved the wilderness, and proved, over and over again, that material obstacles were vulnerable before indomitability of spirit; or that if the impassive hostility of nature cost a man his life, how dearly he gave it was a legacy to fortify later comers. Such an ethic was probably an unconscious response to the conditions men knew on the prairies, for it seemed to be one in which all had a share. More deliberate codes of behavior had their flaws. There was a technique of bankrupt payment of debt which was regarded as perfectly legal by both debtor and creditor; and it had a savage morality. The debtor, unable to pay his debt in money, was privileged to grant "a stripe for a dollar" to his creditor, who tied him to a tree, and lashed him once for every dollar that was uncollectible. It was a public ordeal; a public feast; a strictly regarded form of settlement, which bought a license for hurt and yielded the obscure enjoyment attendant upon the spectacle of pain when sanctioned by numbers of men present, all guilty as witnesses. This, a hundred years ago, during what might be called America's Middle Ages, a period of great preparations for greater discoveries.

Proceeding through new country, Gregg and his companies

named its features and created a living map, by likeness and landmark and growth . . . Mustang Spring, Dove Pond, Hackberry Grove, Bluff Creek, Fired-Prairie Creek. Raised to the dignity of capital letters on a piece of rag paper where their course crawled forth from the pen, those places became realities to other people than just those who first saw them. Gregg's map of the prairies was long regarded as the best one available.

THE INDIANS

In addition to systematic chapters which close *Commerce of the Prairies* with descriptions of Indian life, Gregg composed many an incidental passage about these citizens of the plains. The detail of first interest is that though the traders could speak with Indians only by signs, there was perfect understanding. The will to communicate was enough. If everybody had been as forbearing and sympathetic and unafraid as Gregg was, much of the Indian trouble might never have happened. He describes an Indian encounter in the early pages of the book, and dryly presents a picture of the excitement of the travelers—their apprehension; their confusion; the amateur strategies among the company who would direct the artillery; the wretched condition of the traders' arms—all perfectly understandable in the tradition of Indian savagery with which all these Americans were imbued; and their fears move us when we remember what they must have felt. On the other hand, he describes the Indians in their approach—their sounds in voice and drum; their hundreds of men and women pressing closer all the time, and exhibiting arms of battle, and by mere strangeness, concealing their real intentions. The traders finally must threaten and show strength; they draw up their battle line, and with fife and drum, march toward the main group of Indians in the military menace which among military peoples had always been understood. But not this time. The Indians "seemed far more delighted than frightened with this strange parade and music . . . and perhaps looked upon the whole movement rather as a complimentary salute than a hostile array."

This charming blunder could seem to suggest a most adequate sophistication in the owners of the plains, and if its related history were not so tragically full of battle scenes, it could be regarded as an ironic comedy of the social life of the frontier. The plain truth seems to be that on most such early occasions the Indians neither desired nor expected to fight, for they were at ease and at home, even with strangers, who after all were simply other people. But few enough traders saw the Indians as people, and bothered to seek that understanding which would have good consequences; using instead the only arguments they were independently masters of—the eloquent finalities of bullets.

Gregg saw the Indians as people. He saw that they liked to trade, and that if they'd been treated right in trading relations, much misery might have been saved. "The Santa Fe caravans have generally avoided every manner of trade with the wild Indians, for fear of being treacherously dealt with . . . This I am convinced is an erroneous impression; for I have always found that savages are much less hostile to those with whom they trade, than to any other people. They are emphatically fond of traffic, and being anxious to encourage . . . those with whom they trade, they are generally ready to defend them against every enemy." Gregg wasn't afraid of anything he encountered on the prairies, including Indians. ". . . In the common trait of hospitality to strangers all the western tribes are alike distinguished. The traveller who is thrown upon their charity, is almost universally received and treated with the greatest kindness; and, though they might pilfer him to the skin, and even place his person in jeopardy, *if he shows want of confidence in them*, [my italics] and endeavors to conceal his effects, yet his property is generally secure when under their charge; they appear to consider a breach of confidence one of the greatest crimes."

In other words, Gregg evidently found that if good manners and self-respect dictated the trader's attitude toward the Indians, there was no more to be afraid of than among any population back home. We may accept this testimony of his because we know how precise and fair he always was in matters of factual observation. He was certainly no Rousseau, avowing the fashionable sentiment with which any inhabitants of the wilderness were indulged. He weighed their beliefs with the leverage of his own culture, and of course concluded that many of them were absurd, and gently compared Indians in this respect with "many grandmothers in backwoods life [who] delight in recounting the extraordinary apparitions, transmigrations, sorceries, etc., which they pretend to have witnessed." And then he said—not giving credence, but at least the dignity of tolerance, to the Indian point of view: "If you tell an Indian that such things are absurd and impossible, he is apt to answer, 'It may be so with the white man, but how do you know it to be impossible with the Indian? You tell us many strange things which happened to your fathers—we don't contradict them though we believe such things never happened to the red man.' " Gregg was of course not fetched by this; yet it seems characteristic of his interest in the whole truth that he recorded not only his argument but the Indian's, with its extraordinary delicacy and good breeding.

He had his alarms, like any traveler, of course; and when necessity demanded, he fought and tried to kill and save what was his in fact and in responsibility. But there is nowhere evidence of hatred or injustice in his relations with the Indians. He recorded in his diary and later rewrote for his book an experience, a typical Indian alarm; and from it, we know now what it was like to be awakened by the cry of "Indians! Indians!" on a night when a cold rain was followed by snow before dawn.

"—the shrill sound of a species of whistle used by the Pawnees and the croak clattering of Indian tongues." So that is what it sounded like, "a croak clattering," when Indians made hubbub and attack. The traders fought back in the snowy darkness, firing only at the direction of the noise or flash of the Indians' guns. It kept up for two hours; then it was over, the Indians were gone, the rain and snow continued into daylight, accompanied by a very cold wind . . . There were no losses.

Gregg recorded curious bits of information that more formal histories would submerge and dehumanize. Indian moccasins of different tribes were differently made, and when you came upon Indian footprints across the prairies, there was "always a palpable difference in the tracks."

He never saw a bald Indian.

The eyebrows and eyelashes of the Indians were plucked out. "A 'brave' will spend as much time at his toilet as a French belle in the adjustment of his ornaments—his paint, trinkets, beads and other gewgaws." He always had his mirror with him, and his tweezers, "whether of a fold of tin, of hardened wood, or of spirally twisted wire," and as fast as any hair showed anywhere on his body or face he plucked it out, as unbecoming to a warrior.

If there was much that was outlandish, even to his view, with its curious blend of the dispassionate and the sympathetic, Gregg saw also much about the human culture of the prairie citizens that was fabulous and almost poetic. In giving a description of a great Comanche marksman he was touching the springs of poetry, that raw material of prodigy from which epics are born. Gregg and the Comanche sat side by side on their horses, watching the droll society of prairie dogs, when the Indian aimed an arrow at a little dog who sat fifty or sixty paces distant:

The animal was almost entirely concealed behind the hillock which encompassed the structure of his apartment, so that the dart could not reach it in a direct line; but the Indian had resort to a manoeuvre which caused the arrow to descend with a curve, and in an instant it quivered in the body of the poor little quadruped. The slayer only smiled at his feat, while we were perfectly astounded. There is nothing strange in the rifleman's being able to hit his mark with his fine-sighted barrel; but the accuracy with which these savages learn to shoot their feathered missiles, with such random aim, is almost incomprehensible. I had at the same time drawn one of Colt's repeating pistols, with a view of paying a similar compliment to another dog; when, finding that it excited the curiosity of the chief, I fired a few shots in quick succession, as an explanation of its virtues. He seemed to comprehend the secret instantly, and, drawing his bow once more, he discharged a number of arrows with the same rapidity, as a palpable intimation that he could shoot as fast with his instrument as we could with our patent fire arms. This was not merely a vain show: there was more of reality than romance in his demonstration.

This is a plain factual account of a marvelous feat. But it is something beyond that, too. It is a celebration of the most vital skill there was in that Indian world; and to praise that was to praise life, for it was what insured life, and such a thing touched the obscure but powerful and heartening roots of all such themes in primitive literature.

Through memories in such history the Indian makes his legacy to our inheritance of the American arts.

THE ANIMALS

Aside from the cordial observances which his period dictated in matters of sentiment, Josiah Gregg made few sentimental gestures. There was a dryness to his character which precluded that. It is all the more appealing, then, when occasionally, in his calmly articulate fashion, he made an observation which from someone else would degenerate into sentimentality. We think particularly of the passage in his book where he considered animals as *companions* on the prairie. How charming to mention this in a moment of natural history. Animals "constitute so considerable a portion of the society of the traveller who journeys among them, that they get to hold somewhat the same place in his estimation that his fellow-creatures would occupy if he were in civilization." This was the opinion of a man who held his animals in good favor for more than merely utilitarian reasons, and was probably made livelier by the solitude of humans in the grassy ocean. It would be amusing and natural to credit the patient animals who pulled the wagons and bore the riders with almost an ability to comprehend what they were doing. Anybody who has a feeling for dogs and horses will understand this without any trouble. Anybody who has made a habit of observing the behavior of animals, when life is at some time likely to depend on understanding this behavior, will end by admiring as well as using them.

The animals encountered on the prairies came in for detailed description, a fine catalogue of game which stirs some response in even the least of huntsmen . . . the mustang, the gray wolf with his "long and doleful buglenote," the coyote ("like ventriloquists, a pair of these will represent a dozen distinct voices —will bark, chatter, yelp, whine, and howl in such a variety of note, that one would fancy a score of them at hand"), the elk, the deer, the black bear, the antelope ("I have seen dogs run after this animal, but they would soon stop and turn about, apparently much ashamed of being left so far behind"), the prairie dog, the rattlesnake, the owl, the horned frog, the wild turkey, the prairie hen, the partridge, the bee ("proverbial precursor of the Anglo-American population . . . the aborigines used to say, they knew the whites were not far behind when bees appeared among them")—and above all, of course, the buffalo.

Gregg gave a rich account of these most romantic and mourned of prairie animals: how they were hunted, their bewilderment under attack, their indifference to bullets and slaughter unless they could see or smell the hunter, their character with its odd innocent lumbering ways, their vulnerability when quiet, and, all out of proportion to their size, their susceptibility to defeat. "Even the largest droves (the opinion of some travellers to the contrary notwithstanding), though in the wildest career, are easily turned from their course by a single man who may intercept their way. I have crouched in the tall grass in the direct route of a frighted gang, when, firing at them on their near approach, they would spread in consternation to either side. Still," he said in a characteristic mixture of moderation and eloquence, "still their advance is somewhat frightful—their thundering rumble over the dry plain—their lion-like fronts and dangling beards—their open mouths and hanging tongues—as they come on, puffing like a locomotive engine at every bound, does at first make the blood settle a little heavy about the heart."

In the diary which contributed an episode to the later finished book, there is a note on a Comanche guide who came and told Gregg that there were three bull buffalo over a hill, and might he go and kill one? His employer said he was to limit himself to one. Says the diary, "He promised he would try to kill but one, and set out; but when he got in pursuit of his favorite game, he could not restrain himself, and soon dispatched the 3 [that is, sent them bounding], and observed to one of his comrades, that had he not feared injuring the horse he would have killed all three."

Here it is again, as attested to in countless other documents—this zest for slaughtering the buffalo. What induced it? The massiveness of the animal? His strange speed in flight? His unexpected docility? The accidental aspect of menace which his heavy low-hung head gave him? Why did men laugh when they saw the buffalo? That they did, a Spaniard noted in 1598. Gregg very strongly condemned the wasteful slaughter, and honorably added, "I regret that I cannot give to my precepts the force of my own example: I have not always been able to withstand wholly the cruel temptation," and went on to describe how he came on a herd of buffalo and needlessly shot several, alarming the members of his party who heard the shots; they came galloping, fearing that the sounds meant an Indian fracas. He said, too, that the mustangs of the plains were as idly and willfully destroyed by travelers.

Also in the diary he recorded an odd bit of animal behavior. "The first appearance of spring grass sets animals crazy—they will leave other food to seek after the few sprouting shoots, which begin to peep out of the ground. A horse or mule will thus almost starve with abundance of corn lying by him."

It is another such fact as has a kernel of poetry in it: how a poor dumb beast will respond to the elemental rebirth of spring, and lose his paltry wits, and starve moonily after the tender shoots, alongside a plenty of winter food. But the diarist recorded also a cure for this behavior; the poetry of folly is succeeded by the prose of husbandry: "Therefore, to force them to eat, we resolved on forming a large corral in which to pen and feed them."

He mentioned in the book a pastoral incident which the diary recorded first: "On the night of the 13th [March 1840] it blew an extraordinarily cold N. western all night. Our sheep and goats took a stampede and fled with the wind across the Llano Estacado and we were never able to find them." In this passage there seems to me an engaging elegance, that delicately hooved little herd inspired by agreement, shifting into the direction of the wind and fleeing before it into the darkness and the freedom of the great mesa . . .

And "Oh," he exclaimed elsewhere in the diary, tried sorely by the experience of crossing a quagmire, "what mulish animals are mules!"

Thus, the traveler's dependence upon animals for progress and sustenance, and even for wanton sport, justified all the attention Gregg gave them. What he called the "prairie mythology" had a celebrated animal in it, too, a milk-white mustang stallion, of whom legend was eloquent in all quarters of the West. Nobody ever really *saw* him, but everybody had tales to tell about him, and each locality claimed him as its own: "The trapper celebrated him in the vicinity of the northern Rocky Mountains; the hunter, on the Arkansas, or in the midst of the Plains; while others have seen him pacing at the rate of half a mile a minute on the borders of Texas. It is hardly a matter of surprise, then, that a creature of such ubiquity should never have been caught."

That grand empire of space . . . what would finally conquer it? Mobility, speed, and endurance. The terms of that time would naturally hit upon a horse. This hero, like all others, projected a dream, an unconscious demand, and answered it with man's common poetry of belief.

THE NEW MEXICANS

And now we have crossed the prairie ocean, and have come to harbor at Santa Fe. A whole new society is open to description. What is the method our author is likely to pursue? Why, the scientific method, which served him so well on the plains, in discerning the spirit and quality of the land, the air, the animals, the Indians who were so guiltless of civilization as to seem almost animal themselves, and the devices and dodges of successful travel—in short, prairie culture. Why was this method so successful in these tasks? Because the materials upon which it worked were so fresh, had no challengeable likeness to the frontier society, required no *judgments* derived from an assiduously acquired background of Puritan education, such as flavored polite American life in the early half of the century. And upon what body of material did this method encounter its first, if not its only, defeat? The life and manners of the New Mexicans. And how? Through an observation failing in sympathy, however keen and accurate it might have been. And why? Because of a lack of humor in the historian, partly, and partly because of the common bleakness with which Nordic peoples so often regard their Latin fellows.

For Gregg in his scrupulous catalogue of ways among the New Mexicans of the 1830s never caught the spirit of those people. It is possible to agree with some of his criticisms; but it is the first time he failed to pursue his description of a problem to its cause. Temperamentally this was beyond him, in the case of that volatile, irresponsible, languid, simple, and joyful population. They offended everything about him that was formal, enlightened, and rational, and in his description of them we see in full cry the dislike of the tidy man for the untidy one. This sort of little difference is often apt to cause a deeper breach than a more serious failing.

But it should be said, too, that very few of the early Anglo-Saxon travelers to New Mexico showed any more perception than Gregg in appreciating the valuable qualities of the inhabitants. It is true that civil life, as Americans had known it, was merely parodied in the New Mexican version of the nineteenth century. It is true that education was primitive and privilege abused. It is true that the simplest arts and crafts were awkwardly practiced, and that in architecture "the people do not seem to have arrived at any great perfection." Gambling was a public scandal, and justice was a farce, and the most advanced of the residents were still "pompous" in their style of dress and accoutrement. As for their religion, it was seen and dismissed as a bundle of "superstitions." There was "no part of the civilized globe, perhaps, where the Arts have been so much neglected, and the progress of Science so successfully impeded as New Mexico." And "in nothing [was] the deplorable state of things already noticed made more clearly manifest, than in the absence of a public press." The inhabitants were cowards, their morals were deplorable, and their content with ignorance was scandalous. There was perhaps only one saving feature about the whole wretched province. "Salubrity of climate is decidedly the most interesting feature in the character of New Mexico."

It is a damaging bill of complaints.

But because it was so complete, and so readable, and so unconsciously typical of the prevailing American taste of the time, Gregg's account brought the first hint of the culture of the Western Latins to the United States. What it told, it told with energy and in a familiar tongue—yet it was generally wrong at the core of its ideal purpose, which was to interpret that culture as ably and fairly as the author interpreted the prairie culture. But his very wrongness partakes of a quality of character so genuinely his that, for our purposes in catching the gleams of his reflected life in his book, we value it for its very perversity.

It often seems that if the scientific attitude has a flaw, it is its failure to perceive human character with sympathy. You may adduce all the clinical evidence in the world about a given human subject, and it will add up to a column of statistics and nothing more unless it is examined with warmth and sympathy. Time and again, as later episodes of his chronicle showed, Gregg was wrong about people, judged them too hastily, and on many occasions recorded his change of mind, as was like him. We have seen plenty of proof of how he was in love with nature: the land and its features; the physical world, its phenomena and its laws. Gregg was a cool customer, anyway, except where his irascibilities were touched; and then he had the slightly comic passion of the moral zealot. It is fair to claim that what he saw in New

Mexico offended his moral sense, which had been formed by the dispassionate rationalism which was our early cultural temper, formed by the twin attributes of New England's conscience and the frontier's tenacity.

Now face this view of life with the spectacle of a land so inaccessible that its human ways might have seemed to enact a dream of a life long ago left behind by social evolution; so beautiful in its natural elements that man's vanity had ceased laboring to challenge it with pretentious works; so capricious in its tolerance of man that the simplest terms of life seemed grateful and adequate; so steeped in the twin religions of the Indian and the Spaniard that, despite human errors of administration, they seemed to afford a genuine spiritual interpretation of life to their adherents; so sun-blessed that Latins were at home there —imagine these contrasts, and Gregg's failure to "see" the New Mexicans will not be amazing. There was simply a profound disparity between his idea of amenity and the Latin's. Nowhere is this more sharply dramatized than in his remarks about the Catholic Church, which he called exploiter of the people and propagator of superstition, omitting to recall that if the branch of civilization, as he meant it, was in the least discernible in New Mexico, even as a precariously tenacious seedling in a crevice of Indian rock, then it was the Church herself who had planted it. So, too—aside from matters of truth and dogma—he missed the emotional appropriateness of Catholicism to the people it informed, and the land it pacified. It was a limitation of his temperament, finally, that with all his goodness and his devotion to describing life wherever he went, he had to savor the *human* climate for some time before he really achieved understanding of it, and, sometimes, tolerance.

For in later years, when his Santa Fe tradership was over, and he had no need to keep his wits about him, and contend when necessary, and drive a bargain, and in general keep the inner aloofness upon which successful business enterprise is based

—when he lived among the Mexicans of Saltillo and tended their needs as a doctor—he found peace and was at home among them: "I have often thought that if I could make myself as easy in American society, I would be willing to live in the United States." If they *were* all knaves and villains, cowards and dupes, then he had forgiven them; but perhaps, all along, he had been wrong . . .

Yet it will not do to say that in laying about him so vigorously, he found no targets to be justly hit. He was appalled at the inequality of justice, which made the bribe of the rich man the almost invariable victor over the wrongly done poor man. In wanting a newspaper, he was wanting public enlightenment. He was simply the first observer to find the lack of, and make a wish for, the presence of those values upon which American life was already building a heritage for the common man. Within his individual scale, he was a symptom of what always happens in the first union of disparate cultures. The differences are then most acutely perceived, and presently they merge, the old energized by the new, with the conscious values of both creating a new fabric of living.

As always, there are glimpses by-the-way of details that struck him as odd or interesting; and from them we catch two hints of image—his, and what he was looking at—in a way that academic history never affords. "In giving directions, these people—in fact, the lower classes of Mexicans generally—are also in the habit of using very odd gesticulations, altogether peculiar to themselves. Instead of pointing with their hands and fingers, they generally employ the mouth, which is done by thrusting out the lips in the direction of the spot, or object, which the inquirer wishes to find out—accompanied by *aquí* or *allí está*." He called this habit "labial gestures," and any Southwesterner will recognize it among the Mexican Americans of today, though he may not know whence it grew: "—from the use of the *sarape*, which keeps their hands and arms perpetually confined."

There was a type of coach, "one of those huge, clumsy, old-fashioned vehicles of Mexican manufacture, so abundant in the southern cities, and often nicknamed 'wheeled tarantulas' . . . The coach alone is a load for two mules, therefore the vehicle is usually drawn by four and sometimes six, and invariably driven by postilions."

He did grant that the inhabitants were polite, even though outlandishly so, e.g.: "In epistolary correspondence, the ratio of respect is generally indicated by the width of the left margin. If the letter is addressed to an equal, about one-fourth of the page is occupied for that purpose; but when extraordinary respect is intended to be shown to a superior, nearly one-half of the page is left a blank. There are other marks of civility and respect peculiar to the country," he added with exasperation, "which among us would be accounted absolute servility."

Mexican rich men often laid up their wealth as ingots of silver in the cellar, so that these often looked like "a winter's supply of firewood."

Most of the New Mexican whiskey was made near Taos, where wheat was cheap.

Of the ruins of the Gran Quivira, he says its style of architecture was superior to anything north of Chihuahua.

"Among the most unpleasant customs of this country is that of the *siesta* or afternoon nap; a species of indulgence in which all classes are prone to share." —Here it is again, that attitude of disdain which arises from a merely accurate account of human doings. This implies that there were no customs which were pleasant; only those with degrees of unpleasantness. To rest from labor during the hottest part of the day in a hot summer was "a species of indulgence."

''SOMEHOW MORE HUMBLE''

An honest book is the shadow of an honest man.

We know from Gregg's book what a colonizer saw, and did, and felt; and from the differences of opinion of a hundred years ago, we may read the value of today's likenesses. In this survey of typical details and qualities of *Commerce of the Prairies*— American facts—we have sampled Gregg's experience in the decade of the 1830's, driving those wagons upon the the prairies which shaped his posterity. It is fair to read between his lines, and join our experience, our memory, with his; for the better we know him in his *magnum opus,* and in the diaries, the better the sense of communion we have with what he was, and did, and described. How keen that sense is in us is the measure of how well later historians do their jobs.

Nothing was too trivial to think about, he seems to have said, after you had noticed it.

He kept notes. It was a settled habit with him, as he had told his brother John. He had a field desk, and ink, and paper bound into little pocketbooks; he had pens, a few instruments, some books; and these were the little links of the broken chain of material possession that he kept by him, for they signified freedom. A few books, and some paper, and things to write with . . . if a man has these things, what on earth else does he need? Owning other things, immovable things, tied you down . . .

If you recorded a fact exactly enough, and that meant exactly as *you* felt about it, it was astonishing how satisfying that could be.

It was also astonishing how—sometimes—by some small drift of idea or color of a word, a fact could really seem almost poetic;

not *elegant,* or *romantical*—the way poetry ought to be, in 1840 —but somehow more humble than that, yet curiously moving. That was probably because a fact was often a reminder; and made you feel again what you felt before. Poetry did this, too, of course.

Where poetry and truth meet: there is always the heart of a human character; and, in literary terms, the source of energy in a great book: and that is what we may call *Commerce of the Prairies.*

III

TO MEXICO

THE DOCTOR

THERE WAS ALWAYS A SCIENTIFIC CAST TO Josiah's thought, and there certainly was a scientist's technique of observation in his records. He had tried being a schoolmaster, a lawyer, a prairie trader, a surveyor. All these were not absorbing enough. They did not seem to make him any the more comfortable. There were many things unanswered. One of the hardest things to understand was perhaps oneself. Why this wretched health? Why this uneasiness in any settled society? Why when he comes home are his resources of health and fortitude so heavily taxed?

The early spring of 1845, at Shreveport, was a lovely season. There was much to observe in the country. The town was five miles away (John had moved again and Josiah was visiting him). It was far enough for a determined hermit. "I cannot even endure our village for more than an hour at a time. I frequently send for the weekly mail to get rid of seeing the streets of Shreveport . . . I see nobody—hearing nothing but the singing of birds, etc." A man always alone by his own choice must spend much time dwelling upon his own situations. That Gregg did so is clear from his letters and diaries. He is preoccupied with his poor health, which of course made it seem all the poorer. The sympathetic and intelligent brother with whom he spent so many interludes between "enterprises" wrote a fine letter after Josiah's death in which we find many clues to a complex temperament, which when it was happy was not happy in an ordinary way. Over and over John records that Josiah would become restless on returning home. Nothing suited his taste or was adapted to his genius. Josiah himself was at a loss to explain this. But that he realized how his state of health was involved there is plenty of evidence. His scientific knack was visible early in his life. John wrote of him that as a child he had often said, "I can't pass by anything I don't understand."

His next important move may have been dictated not only by his scientific tastes but also by a desire to further his understanding of that which had baffled him so when he desisted for a moment from his pursuit of the active physical life to which, on first notice, he appeared so ill adapted. For in the autumn of 1845 he went to Louisville, Kentucky, to enter a medical college to study for the degree of doctor of medicine. He stayed a little over a year, hearing six lectures a day, each an hour long. Evidently he was not enrolled as a regular student—this middle-aged man with so many determining experiences behind him. But he was granted his degree under the honorary convention at the commencement in March 1846. Study for the doctor's degree in medicine was then not so universally standardized as now, and often a doctor was made simply through the serving of an apprenticeship under a practicing physician. But it must have been perfectly plain to the faculty that Josiah was in every way superior as a candidate for the degree, and by his intelligence and application undoubtedly earned it. The idea of practicing was evidently never very important to him. He wrote his brother that he would certainly never use the title doctor unless he *did* practice.

It is interesting, in line with our notice of his unsociable ways, that he elected Louisville as a place for study because he knew nobody there. After he was there for a while, he wrote home that he hated meeting up with someone he knew who introduced him to many acquaintances—including professors. He said it would interfere with his "grand object" in coming here—his studies. But not long after, he seemed much attached to some of his new friends on the faculty. What barriers of constraint and acute self-consciousness must have surrounded him at first, in any new situation.

He did not feel very well throughout that winter. At one point he was about to quit his studies and leave Louisville because he felt so wretched. ("I am now in no condition to study.") Everything around him was colored by his state. ". . . though I have said nothing on the subject, I fancy *que los señores profesores* [that the professorial gentlemen] are becoming a little more distant, as though they thought I might expect favors; I cannot beg of them, that is certain. Beg *honors* of such a corps!" (Through elegance or embarrassment he often used foreign phrases in his letters and attempted a wry jocosity by the liberal salting of his lines with quotation marks. It is the kind of indirection a shy person making an effort would resort to.) But the same professors did give him his honorary degree, and regardless of how he scorned them, he did accept it. "As for my studies, I have got on badly, what between trouble of mind and ill health." —What is significant here is the conjunction. He, in his time, separated health of mind from health of body. To us, in our time, they seem interrelated. "I could never live under my oppression of spirits anywhere in the U.S. where I would be liable to continued annoyance."

ALIEN ABROAD

This refrain is so frequent that we cannot help countering it with the question, Why? Why didn't society enclose him comfortably? He was literate, well acquainted with polite observances; indeed, he was sometimes very stiff about them. To judge from his photographs (of which there are exceedingly few), he was personable, with a look of vitality and keenness about the eyes, which were dark, and deeply porched by fine brows. His face was rather pointed, revealing its bony formation frankly. His hair was dark and abundant. He had a well-shaped mouth, at rest in a reserved expression. Since he habitually bought the best quality of merchandise, it is likely that he was always well groomed. An engraving in the early editions of his book shows a figure of medium height standing on a knoll with an Indian guide, watching, across a deep plain where prairie wagons are encamped, the approach of a great band of Comanche warriors. In the text Gregg says he ascended this knoll with the guide, and the engraved figure is presumably his. He is wearing a plainsman's wide-brimmed hat and a knee-length coat belted close to the waist, hung with huge pockets. He wears his trousers outside his boots. He is gesturing to the Indian guide to signal the approaching warriors with his white blanket. This miniature engraved figure is not a portrait in the ordinary sense; but it is a glimpse of a man in a moment of truth, however conventionalized by the graphical idiom of nineteenth-century illustration. What it confirms somehow is our sense of his dignity.

"I have no desire to be considered an odd fish," he used to say, according to his brother John. It is a touching admission that he was so considered. He never drank, did not like liquor, was temperate in both food and drink; but he "sometimes would take a glass of spirits with a friend, as it would appear, merely not to be considered *odd*." It is a wistful gesture, the complete solitary reaching out to become one with his fellows. In the curious laws of personality, he was made to *feel* eccentric, and so increasingly, protectively, he *acted* eccentrically, and thus became a "type," a sort of wandering intellectual cartoon among the venturesome men of the Westward period. We may smile at the circumstance, but what remains is admiration for the steadfastness of his essential self, which created his satisfactions out of the hardest materials. Often before, and since, that has been the attribute of genius.

And yet it is hard to blame anyone for misunderstanding him, when we reflect upon his vision of propriety and its inflexibility. He had so little humor in his idle jottings and his formal pages alike that it seems fair to decide even this late that he showed none in his personal dealings. For instance, in his great book, he describes the smoking of the calumet, or peace pipe, with a tribal circle on the prairies; and he behaves as if the act of smoking itself were intrinsically novel—as if it had been unknown to the white races for the previous two and a half centuries. Without humor, then, he says that the pipe passes around the circle of councilmen, which is not necessarily funny —simply interesting. Then he speaks solemnly of the councilmen, "each sending fumid currents upward from the nozzle."

This is no doubt to him an exact description of what happened. But Gregg hated smoking, and the gravity of his description is disdainful, all out of proportion to the familiarity of the act. What a contradictory man; how interesting to catch this dry flavor from the same man who is moved to deep feeling by other acts of prairie life. We begin to detect his curious insulation against human preoccupations, frailties, oddnesses. It is tempting to think up an explanation of this remoteness in him, which often seems like a lack of sympathy. Perhaps it is fair to excuse him by saying that he was harsh in self-judgment, and disciplined a poor body and an unsocial spirit until he felt their human claims reduced to unimportance. His severity upon others might thus have been induced first by the habit of severity with himself.

He was that anomaly in society, the one who appears to betray his kind by standing apart and observing them; and for him they inevitably hold a sort of uneasy derision. He was neither wholly a trader, nor an artist, nor a scientist, nor a physical man, but a thoughtful combination of all these; and on the frontier, where judgments were simple and likenesses were apt to be crudely reckoned, he was a puzzling creature. He was not even an out-and-out fraud, a pretentious "professor" whose intellectual claims could be howled down in good-humored hazing. There is evidence that Gregg's very abilities, however much their use gratified him alone, exposed him to annoyance.

If society does that to him, he may strike back with "critical intelligence" and enjoy the bleak satisfactions of lonesome superiority. Does this explain why he should be so eternally insulted by steamboatmen, soldiers, lady hotel keepers, frontier travelers on the trail, the thousand and one thoughtless opportunists who were doing their share in the frontier life he was describing so truly and coolly?

He was, among them, alien.

They were doing jobs and butting against obstacles and lending their bodies and their shrewdnesses to the task of conquest, and of surviving it. All this time he was acting in one further dimension of effectiveness—he was analyzing, reasoning, recording. He was observing the conditions of natural life through which other men passed with shorter sight. He was the theorist, the man of mind, in the West-rolling procession of men of action. To him the highest act of a man was *to understand*. But we all know another kind of man who views with contempt and anger the wresting of knowledge from the frontal experience of life, and who tries to punish any other who would do it. This was expressed in the hazing of the frontier. Gregg would have been at home in New England; he could have talked with Emerson and Thoreau. But he was torn between the freedom of the prairies, where he was accountable only to his thoughts— where, indeed, they had no audience—and the need for sharing these thoughts. His book is the solution of this conflict. Having no sustained contact with society, for whatever reason, he *wrote* to it, and secured himself a posterity, of which he surely never thought except in terms of what later men would think of the trustworthiness of his work.

"SERVICE TO MY COUNTRY"

In March 1846, the new Dr Gregg is on his way home and has stopped in St. Louis to do some shopping—a few polite gifts for the family, an album for Eliza, a volume of poems for Miss Kitty, the works of Hannah More and Mrs Ellis, a little picture primer for the baby, and a "dozen ordinary primers . . . for Puss and the babe to learn to read in." Having not much money, he got these literary items in exchange for copies of his own work. He bumped into some old friends, J. T. Cleveland and his wife, who were "very kind indeed," although "they want to *casarme con una viuda* [marry me to a widow], an elegant miniature portrait painter, who says she would be 'delighted' with a life on the Prairies—but they 'can't quite come it.'" Eluding the gifted widow, he hurried home to Independence, with thoughts of the prairies in his head, after a whole winter in the doubly constricted society of an American city and an academic institution.

He soon made arrangements to set sail on the plains with his old friend and partner, Colonel Owens, but delays occurred;

goods from the East failed to arrive, and scarlet fever broke out in the family of his sister and brother-in-law, the James Lewises. It was a miniature epidemic. Eight of the family finally came down with it. The neighbors were terrified; "few offered help," and Gregg "was compelled to remain sitting up half of the nights till I left."

But life in this inland port of the prairie sea was already exciting. "The emigration this spring to California or Oregon will be immense." He saw it; he recorded something of its stirring significance between the lines of his diary: "—6000 souls, with 1000 wagons, moving Westward across the great Prairies during the present summer from this part of our frontier." It is like an intonation, as well as the statement of a fact. To the west lay the future. To the south lay Mexico. But Mexico had been a far country since 1843, when Santa Anna closed the Mexican trade because Americans were sympathetic and helpful to Texas in her border troubles. News from Mexico came to Independence, Missouri, earlier by way of New York, two thousand miles away, than by way of Santa Fe, eight hundred miles across the plains.

But this was 1846, and the United States was at war with Mexico, and a venture in the Santa Fe trade was likely to be backed up shortly by the United States penetration into the northern Mexican province.

He sent his books, instruments, baggage, and so on, ahead in the wagons of Colonel Owens and set out to overtake them alone a few days later by horse. The whole country was aware of the war. There was a strong sentiment for intervention. A justification was maintained by debates in Congress. When Texas achieved statehood, the nation inherited the border difficulties of its newest state. Gregg observed that he was with President Polk in the matter, and in a Macaulayian sentence of symmetry and elegance remarked, "for though, when the subject was first agitated, I had my misgivings as to the consequences and policy, and also thought the rights of Mexico should be to some degree respected, the discussion of the matter has dissipated the first difficulty, and the deportment of Mexico the second."

Arkansas and Missouri raised volunteers.

It was a time when citizens felt privileged to serve. Gregg was approached by Colonel Yell, Member of Congress from Arkansas, to go along to Texas with the Arkansas volunteer regiment as a kind of expeditionary aide, whose knowledge of the country, people, and Mexican language would be useful. But the request was not very specific as to his duties or rank, and since he had already sent his possessions out on the prairies, he left to overtake the wagons on the plains.

Shortly afterward, as the wagon train was moving overland on the trek, it was overtaken by the owner, Colonel Owens, who arrived from Independence, bringing another appeal to Gregg, this time from Senator Sevier, also of Arkansas, urging him to join the Chihuahua army; and he decided to go. This second letter "substantially warranted me an 'honorable and profitable' situation." He took up whatever luggage he could "conveniently carry on a horse, with my sextant, etc.," and turned back to Missouri—yet if his horse had not happened to run away, he says, he "probably should not have returned but for this casualty; though my horse was brought back to me after I got everything ready to start back, and the wagons of Col. Owens had started on." He went home and waited for more definite mail from Washington. Such matters as his exact status, his rank, his pay, had not been discussed. To a precisionist, this was exasperating.

Nothing came in decent season, so he decided to "start south this morning [Monday, 22 June 1846]; for that is the point where I had the greatest hope of making my humble service of some use. The sacrifice I make on this occasion is certainly very great, for I was compelled to permit my baggage, books, and all my preparations of outfit and convenience for the tour, continue across the prairies with Col. Owens. However, I shall feel amply compensated for all my privations and labors, if my present tour turns out to be of any service to my country."

He was out to do his best; but his services would be the cause of irritation on both his side and the army's. He was wasted upon a job that was neither wholly civilian nor wholly military. He was hazed by the soldiers, and his intelligence was affronted by the poor administration of the high command. The war was a tragicomedy, enacted upon a barren stage under the pouring light of the desert sky. Nothing ever seemed to get done; and yet, one day, the forces found themselves arrayed for a vast engagement; and the wasteful, dreary, inconclusive months were forgotten; and the policy of a continent was secured in battle at Buena Vista.

PRELUDE TO BATTLE

"This is a singular warfare we are waging, is it not?" he asked in one of his letters to the editors of the *Louisville Journal* in 1846. From his point of view, the whole thing was an accumulation of irritations, inefficiencies, and humiliations.

Gregg was rarely the man to temper his judgments, either of himself or of others. He had survived the hardships of the plains, during that decade when the Santa Fe trade was the prosaic instrument of the national design. He was forty years old, and felt, and looked, much older, in the robust and thoughtless company of the United States army in Mexico, whom he was accompanying as what: guide? translator? interpreter? The point of his status was never cleared up, although he was supposed to receive "the pay and perquisites of a Major." If he felt like an outsider, he certainly talked and wrote like one. His experiences with the army invading Mexico left a bitter taste. He was genuinely eager to be of service. He was ready, like a patriotic American, to march with a well-disciplined force under brilliant officers to a rapid and humane and, above all, efficient conclusion of the Mexican adventure. What he met with was altogether different. Everywhere he turned, someone or something served to bring out his most acidulous opinions. The war was to be fought, here, on this map? Then why was it not done exactly so, on the ground itself?—that baked and reptilian desert, where few men have subdued the natural world according to their orderly designs. General John Ellis Wool, first of all, the commanding officer, was unpopular with "at least ninety-nine hundredths of the troops he commanded. Ergo: could all have been right" with the state of affairs? Wool may have been "an amiable gentlemanly man; yet I fear rather crabid and petulant, and perhaps . . . old-womanish—more efficient in minutiae and details than in grand and extensive operations."

That was what was wanted: "grand and extensive operations," and the war would simply not live up to them. Endless sky, the grit of hot sand, an amateur army, the growing pains of the nation, the vanity of men contending with sense. General Wool moved about the town with staff and guard of twenty mounted dragoons with drawn sabers, a spectacle which Gregg did not like. The other officers, too, were "petulant," "out of their element." They quarreled, they resigned, they wrote lengthy "reports" and justified themselves, they bore themselves haughtily, even Captain Albert Pike, though he deserved "to stand decidedly 'number one' in point of talent and acquirements," even Pike, on the way to Chihuahua, later, was very remiss of his men's comfort, and was sternly caught at it and duly noted in the evening's session with the bound notebooks.

A certain Colonel Hamtramck was even worse than General Wool at pomposity, a quality which was just a disguise: "The fact is, any man with a fair degree of cunning and management, who is abjectly subservient, and will use a sufficiency of flattery, will hardly fail to gain a great influence over the general's weak mind." As for General Shields and General Butler, the one "is a military monomaniac—crazy—his head addled by his elevation . . . one of the veriest *military* simpletons," and the other, "as a military man, though brave as need be, no doubt, he is rather imbecile." Josiah had occasion to smart under "the rudeness of Gen. Lane and more especially his aide . . . who, to make up for his ignorance and want of talent, put on an air of insupportable presumption—at the same time inclining to treat me as his 'orderly' while I was gratuitously interpreting for them. The low grade in which interpreters are held, and the low class of people, in fact, generally engaged as such, is one reason why I have refused to accept this office, even though at a high salary."

He said that he, himself, would never solicit an army commission from the President, it being beneath his dignity. However, he added, with the offhand sort of hint so binding to relative or friend, that his brother John might take steps, if he liked. As to rank, it was now too late to satisfy him with the rank, as well as the perquisites, of a major: "but *Lieut. Colonel* I should be very well pleased with." He underlined it to make it perfectly sure, and saw himself suitably uniformed; but nothing came of this delicate intrigue, even after he left General Wool to join the staff of General W. P. Butler; and when he left Butler, eventually, Josiah refused the pay accrued and due to him, for the very Greggian reason that although yes, he had earned it, he disdained to accept it because he had never been given a definite appointment. A propriety so fierce, so baffling to the very spirits it intended to educate with an austere rebuke, must have appeared merely cranky to them.

He was tempted many times to give up his association with the army and set out as a freelance reporter of the fantastic campaign. His effects—books, instruments, records—had gone on to Santa Fe with Colonel Owens and from there had been taken down to Chihuahua, where they now awaited him. He was spoiling to get to Chihuahua; to be free of this military society in which he was so uneasy; to recover his possessions; to know again the consuming duty of observing the country, accountable to no one. But there were delays. One of them, as it turned out, was worth the bother.

BATTLE PIECE

At last, for a time, all was forgiven that infinitely puzzling army. For when the long time of preparation was somehow done with, and the foes met by the hacienda of Buena Vista at the foot of that mountain which looked so beautiful at times, Gregg was full of fellow feeling and ardent sympathy with the very soldiers whom he had judged with a sniff, and who had hazed him back, in their cruder way. The battle, he wrote to John, was "that glorious but awful affair." It had been coming for days—a Mexican spy in the town kept reporting to Gregg, and there is an innocent sense that the town evidently knew of the battle plans from day to day.

When the day came and the troops were moving to their stations, the wagons rattled so that the Mexicans thought the noise came from artillery fire.

Josiah was there, riding a horse all in and around the battle, maintaining himself "on high and commanding points . . . so as to have a view of all the operations." He was in great danger from musket fire throughout, with his calm, orderly, recording eye in the midst of the confused action. As usual, his factual net took in details which were the prosaic seedlings of poetry, of feeling. He heard the United States soldiers greet a Mexican cannonade with "hearty yells," and the words suddenly resume their original meanings, and in the smoky blue battle air we see again the toiling little figures by the batteries, and we feel the thudding valor of their hearts, which saved a day and swayed a century.

Josiah wrote several accounts of the battle. He described it to John by letter, and he wrote more formal accounts which appeared in the newspapers back home. Even now, his description reads with excitement and awe, ennobled with the emotion which a less embarrassed and cynical age than that following Korea and Vietnam felt free to associate with patriotism. In the hand-to-hand warfare of Gregg's time, pity was still a right of the victor; and he described not only the suffering of the defeated Mexican troops but also the mercies of the United States soldiers to the wounded enemy after the battle was over. He saw his compatriots tending the wounds of the Mexicans on the battlefield, and giving them water, for which they cried. He found and helped to bury his old friend Colonel Yell, of Arkansas, who had persuaded him in the first place to turn back from an expedition out on the plains and join the Arkansas Volunteer Regiment. From the smoke and loss of the battle, a new continent was struggling to arise. Gregg had intimations of it. The active war, in effect, was over, though much yet remained to be concluded with the withdrawal of troops. Patience? Patience was never one of Josiah's virtues. Possibly the analytical intelligence cannot wait, once it has the answer in mind. But when the answer took form and was paid for dearly in flesh and blood, then the long argumentative months, the uncouth maneuvers, the rude manners of campaigning soldiers were forgiven; and at the Battle of Buena Vista, Gregg admired as heroes the officers and men whose other values and purposes had not reached any sympathy in him.

THE MISSOURI
INDEPENDENT

After the battle came an opportunity to make the trip to Chihuahua. A Santa Fe trader named Collins, now interpreter to Doniphan's regiment, had come from that city bringing dispatches from Colonel Doniphan, who had marched down from Santa Fe and was now in control of north-central Mexico. Collins was about to return to Doniphan after Buena Vista, and Gregg was eager to attach himself to the party and reclaim his effects in Chihuahua. It would be a suitable arrangement. Collins's party was to be escorted by troops under the command of Captain Pike, "decidedly 'number one.'" There was only one obstacle, and it had to do with vanity: to go with Collins and Pike, Gregg had first to obtain official permission through petition to General Wool. To ask a favor of this miniature Napoleon indeed posed a struggle between pride and utility. Pride lost, but haughtily.

He made his request in a personal interview. The general had been reading the papers, all along. He was smarting under the published criticisms by his irritable guest, and, worse, he even had heard that Gregg "was going to write a book." It was a chilling rumor. The general received Gregg with a sense of injury. Dr Gregg bore himself with the mien of justice incorruptible. They conversed. Immediately afterward, Gregg wrote down a report of the meeting. It is plain that, for whatever reason—an eye on posterity in the presence of book writers, or whatever—the general tried to make friends. But Gregg was suspicious, declaring that the general was only angling for admiration and approval. In Gregg's report, Wool does most of the talking, borne on by a torrent of words—"that state of irritability

in which a man has to talk, talk, talk, merely to convince himself
that he is in the right," as Tolstoy said of the original Napoleon.
In any case, the interview ended with permission for Gregg to
set out with Collins and Pike.

Free of his doubtful army connections at last, he started off
on the five-hundred-mile trip through enemy territory to recover
his belongings at Chihuahua. He was fully aware of the dangers
involved, but he was as lofty toward peril as he was toward ignorance.

Even the Mexicans themselves were in danger from Indians,
and the United States troops sometimes had to help. "This is
certainly a novel warfare," wrote Gregg, "fighting and defend-
ing the same people at the same time, and killing those who
would be our allies if we would permit them. True, although at
war with the Mexican *nation*, we have never pretended to hos-
tilize the unarmed citizens, and, under no circumstances, could
we permit the savages to butcher them before our eyes. This dis-
play of a spirit to defend the people against their worst enemies,
the Indians, will, I hope, be attended with good effect."

Gregg had some just and sensible remarks to make on the
subject of military reprisals against enemy nationals. General
Taylor had issued some particularly sharp orders, and Gregg
could see, at the time, how cruel and unjust they were. He took
justice and reason with him wherever he went, or tried to, despite the unreliability of his health and his resultant capacity for
indignation, which was at times boundless. But if he became in-
dignant on his own account more often than was quite dignified,
he also spared no wrath upon those who persecuted others. In his
accounts of the army in Mexico, and of people on the move generally, we get his ethical flavor at its best. He never felt that
the laws of home should be left behind by the traveler, or that
character was a *local* matter.

At Chihuahua he gathered together his belongings, and eyed

Colonel Doniphan's column, which had marched down from Santa Fe, won the Battle of Chihuahua, and was now prepared to march east to join General Taylor.

Gregg joined the column, but of course in his own fashion. One day, under the blazing sun, the soldiers beheld an apparition, which they hailed with incredulity and finally with roars of laughter. It was Dr Gregg, bolt upright in his mule's saddle, with various outlandish accoutrements strapped about him, wearing his habitual expression of disdainful interest, and holding over his head a red silk parasol. Rejuvenating their tired spirits at his expense, the soldiers began to release their wit. Catcalls and remarks, at which he was "a little annoyed as well as amused." He was irked, too, at the "impertinence of the volunteers in other regards. Being constantly employed in collecting botanical specimens, etc.," as he said of himself, the soldiers "must needs know every particular about them . . . often accompanied by taunting and insulting expressions; so that the naturalist has to pass an ordeal in laboring among ignorant people, who are wholly unable to comprehend the utility of his collection."

For Gregg never ceased his scientific labors, and kept making bundles of specimens of Mexican flora to send, fully catalogued, to his friend Dr George Engelmann, of St. Louis. His work was of genuine value; but everywhere his experience in performing it was the same. Among the cheerful, the lusty, the rascally, occasionally criminal, characters of our frontier century, with its necessarily muscular values, he was often regarded as a crank. He did not have the one quality which might have saved such a judgment. It was humor. Now and then a pleasantry gleamed wanly through his careful writing; but nowhere was there a healing gust of laughter, which would have blown away the clouds of irritation he so often knew among people. If we imagine him, severe, correct, careful, at his scientific observation, with a solemnity which ruder men might take for disdainful superiority, it is not hard for us to understand, though we would not justify, their view of him. After all, he gravely recorded that at Castañuela he not only saw a dwarf but measured him.

At Monterrey, he found old General Taylor, and measured him, too, though in words. The general was all dressed up in uniform ("pants, with stripes") for the first time—he always used to wear an old, civilian coat, and to dispense with the striking insignia of his rank. Now he wore epaulettes and had sentries, for the Presidency was a genuine possibility, and he made these grand gestures, said Gregg, as marks of respect for Doniphan's Missourians, whom he had previously reprimanded, and whose arrival must now be an agreeable occasion for them to recall at the polls in the autumn.

Through with the army, and far removed from his old life on the plains, Gregg was readily receptive when Samuel Magoffin, veteran Santa Fe trader, proposed a partnership in an "enterprise," Gregg's familiar term to mean a trading venture. Gregg was to go, now, to Philadelphia, where Magoffin had established large credits, and buy merchandise, which would be shipped to Mexico. It was a pleasing return to the pioneer trade, and he went East in the late spring of 1847. He had barely arrived in New York when word came that Magoffin considered the "enterprise" too great a risk financially and that the deal was off.

"He has done me great injustice," wrote Josiah with restraint, "and caused me immense inconvenience; for I had left most of my baggage at Saltillo, upon the faith of the engagement to return." It meant that he would have to go back after this useless journey to get all his possessions, books, instruments, data.

In New York he tried to see his old friend Bigelow, who was never in; nor did Bigelow respond to any of the notes and cards which Gregg left upon him. The venture was altogether a nuisance, and it was in an attempt to snatch something from the long and expensive journey that Gregg went (by way of Brandywine Springs) to Washington, "with the idea I might obtain some government employ in Mexico." But he was appalled, as a proper citizen, at the state of government affairs. He had a visit with the President, and was "astonished at the evident weakness of Mr. Polk." Making a hard judgment upon the man, at first contact, as he usually did, Gregg withdrew from Washington with almost an air of ceremonial disdain for Polk, feeling that he "would not accept anything at his hands." It was "remarkable that a man so short of intellect should have been placed in the executive chair." And yet, to a democrat, with a small "d," it was not so surprising when it is remembered that Polk had not been elected by the people, who would never have done it, "but by a caucus at Baltimore who rather desire a 'creature' than talent to leave designing politicians a tool."

Gregg started West again, writing several letters on the way to his friend Dr George Engelmann, on botanical matters.

THE ''UNACCOMMODATING''

Always plagued by steamboats and their "unaccommodating" officers—it was his eternal word of censure—he started down the Mississippi. He noted "the great self-importance and commanding tone of the 'mate.' Really, these petty steamboat officers exercise their authority with more 'zest' than a general over thousands!" and "Captains and clerks are unfortunately too often . . . perfect despots within their little floating realm." They were aboard the *Martha Washington*. She went aground several times. A day later (August 27, 1847) he was on board the "small steamer 'Ellen'—a wretchedly mean clerk again." Four days later, "in little stern wheel steamer 'Jim Gilmer.' Another mean clerk!" As for the captain of the S.S. *Telegraph*, "being pretty tipsy, he flew into a great passion."

He had meant to go straight to New Orleans on the great river, and thence direct to Monterrey, but the yellow fever was raging in New Orleans, and he turned aside again to visit the John Greggs at Shreveport. He improved his stay by exploratory wanderings on the Red River and by listening to accounts of the Great Raft which natives had seen, a frontier marvel too extraordinary to omit. Intermittently for some two hundred miles, and continuously for sixty miles, the Red River was once covered with a solid, water-level roofing of logs and vegetation so dense and "so overgrown with timber for many miles, that the traveler might pass over across the river without knowing it." The phenomenon was mentioned by other frontier recorders, including Farnham and Edwin James, though Gregg had "never seen the person who has witnessed such a state of the river." But he declared that Farnham's account was exaggerated. James noted that the water-borne jungle had been blasted out with powder by government agency.

Presently he moved on again, and in New Orleans on September 24 was obliged to glare at "a hotel clerk—Fallon—most surly, unaccommodating and I fear ill-faithed fellow." It was a description, too, of Captain Dubbs of the steamer *Ashland*, on which Gregg sailed for the Brazos from New Orleans in November 1847. It was a preposterous voyage. "This wretched vessel is short and round-bottomed, without keel or cut-water, and therefore would slide over the water sidewise" before the wind. The master was drunk day and night. Unseaworthy, the *Ashland* was almost disabled in the Gulf of Mexico, when the schooner *Miranda*, of New York, was sighted. The miserable passengers of the *Ashland* were joyful at the chance to be taken off; any change would be, they felt, an improvement. The *Miranda* at first refused to take them aboard and sailed away. But before long, she came about and returned, signaling that she would take the passengers, but that the *Ashland*'s boat would have to bring them. This the drunken Captain Dubbs refused to agree to, and the *Miranda,* of New York, resumed her course. Gregg and his fellow victims were in "despair."

It was a really intolerable adventure, taking seventeen days to cover a voyage ordinarily done in four. When at last they dropped anchor off the Brazos, their drunken captain could not make up his mind. First he would, then he wouldn't, put them ashore, pending repairs on the boiler. He finally let them go, and they drew up and signed a bill of complaints against master and vessel, and through its almost spinsterish genius for converting irritation into logical complaint, who wrote it is unmistakable.

Gregg's next embarkation was on the steamer *General Jesup,* with his luggage and a dearborn carriage, up the Rio Grande, and at last, on board the light draft steamer *Oreline,* he found a steamboat captain who passed muster, "a son of the celebrated divine, Rev. Mr. Moffitt," with whom there was no occasion for "a tart repartee," as Josiah sometimes described his own weapon in his endless quarrel with the "unaccommodating" wretches on frontier travel.

At last he was back in Saltillo, after a wearing journey. The United States armies were still in occupation, but everybody was hoping for a signing of the peace treaty before long. When the troops went home, new heroes would go along; and politics would be enlivened by battle cries. He wrote to Bigelow—who had written a "very gratifying letter," so that his apparent indifference in New York was magnanimously forgotten—giving him a cool and balanced view of General Taylor, from whose readiness the home sentiment was roughing out a piece of Presidential timber. Far from the excitements of national politics, Gregg was able to resist the political contagion of the warrior's legend: "—a very clever sort of old fellow, but as to his being a very *great* man—even as a warrior, and much less in every other regard—it is all nonsense to talk about it." However, politics aside, and the enthusiasm of backers discounted, "if the people would let him stand at what he merits, there is no man, whom in his way, I would esteem higher than Gen. Taylor."

"WAYS AND DOINGS"

In the winter and spring of 1847–48, he stayed in Saltillo as a medical practitioner, the only time in which his studies at Louisville were formally applied. His services were enormously popular. Writing to John, he said that his fees had grown steadily month by month, and that his high of over $400 for the month of April could actually have been worth over $5,000 if he had wanted to charge as unfairly as his competitors in the town.

There is a sense that he was happy in Mexico: it was a new country to be looked at, and recorded about, and when he was doing that, he was really alive. The Mexicans were engaging. Was there a possibility that here he might find a society in which he would be at home? Here is what might have been an arch hint:

"Tell Eliza and Kitty that I got pretty 'high in the paper' at Saltillo among the *señoritas*. At least I became 'De biggest boy in all de town' with the belle of the city. I was even invited on visits with her and gallivanted through the streets, with her trailing on my arm. 'That's some,' you'll say, *pero no había más*." ["But there will be no more."]

The accent of dead slang and the flurry of quotation marks, and his embarrassed complacency, all give us the bachelor unaccustomed to romance. Aside from the artistic widow who painted miniatures and who was not averse to a life on the prairies, this was the only reference to relation with women in all his known writings.

He collected the little grains of interest which go to make up any local scene. Gossip of the time does more for its history than solemn tablets. The mountains near Saltillo he called "decidedly romantic and beautiful," and we get a flavor of his period from that usage. There was a horse thief who escaped by joining in the hue and cry of "Stop thief!" and we note how unbroken a lineage sustains rascals in their ingenuity. As for politics, or intrigue, there was a project (October 1848) to form a new and separate republic out of four Mexican frontier states, Tamaulipas, Nuevo León, Coahuila, and Chihuahua, to be called La República de la Sierra Madre. But since there were private adventurers behind it, Josiah objected and would have none of it.

Gregg's medical partner in Saltillo was a Dr G. M. Prevost, and in Josiah's cool, scolding account of him, we can still feel the poor human warmth of folly over a hundred years old: "He unfortunately became in love—desperately so—and what was more remarkable for a man of his intellect, with a little girl (13 years old) without any special beauty or merit—and still less talent and intelligence." The young man was "of rather unusually handsome person." He was swept away from his medical responsibilities by "his high empassioned temperament," and when reproached gave himself "airs of haughtiness and self-importance." Nothing was more distressing to his senior partner than "his utter want of system and order . . . everything in the way of medicines topsy-turvy and in perfect confusion . . ."

To the self-disciplinarian, such an affair could only be exasperating. What a waste of time and attention! He had a better scheme for improving evenings. He got up Spanish classes in Saltillo, to meet in the evenings, to (1) have "social collections"; (2) educate the officers; (3) "break up . . . card parties." He organized his venture ardently; but only a few came, and it perished. In February 1848, at Saltillo, he was turned out of his house by the army, and a Major Howard and "a family of prostitutes" moved in. But he was busy as a doctor, he was happy, and he seemed satisfied. "If I could make myself as easy in American society," he wrote John, "I would be willing to live in the United States."

He was evidently liked by the people, and it seems clear that at last he liked them, although he was always more or less in hot water with the official world, even in Mexico. On one occasion he was held in Guadalajara by the local governor, and was proceeded against by troops, but he felt outlandishly confident of being able "to defeat them with only his servants." But good sense dissuaded him from amateur warfare, and the affair ended with an apology from the proper quarter.

Again and again we run up against a quality in him which in the cool medium of his own words sounds priggish, and which in the more vital medium of his living presence must have obscured his great virtues and services from less thoughtful men than he. (We must not allow the infirmity and impatience of this period of his life to disguise his great achievement as historian of the prairies, and we must remember that the dignity and courage of his last days were yet to come.) If he served science, it must often have seemed that he served it with such indignation that others—all others—did not see the responsibility, and the priority, of the act.

He rarely felt the human climate so sharply as he did meteorology. And yet—such was the honesty of the man—he reported the wise "lecture" which General Almonte gave him (April 12, 1849) on Mexico's comparative infancy in the modern world, and the impatience of the United States. Still, a masquerade which he described, and which, by his own details, we find charming, he called "brutally absurd."

Since he was not feeling too well during this period, his irascibility was that of the invalid, the man who found his resources of body unequal to the wants of his interests and imagination. In visiting the mines of Real del Monte, he was "too weak" to go down ladders to the bottom of deep ravines. "As usually happens to me, the ride out in the stage so disordered my stomach, that I was greatly debilitated for a day or two after." Had he become clumsy and uncertain in his movements? He lost his keys by dropping them somewhere. Bending over a pool, he lost his Colt revolver out of its holster, and saw it vanish in the water. The same thing happened again, and the party he was with impatiently went on without him while he tarried behind, trying to recover the pistol.

But he had plans for examining new lands and finding new specimens. He wrote to his friends about these ideas. One project was to go from Mexico City down to South America, passing over the Isthmus, to explore the outlines of the great continent, going first down the Atlantic side, around Cape Horn, a fabulous land voyage, and then back on the Pacific side up into California, and across to Santa Fe (which was by now a territorial capital), and thence home to the United States. He was forty-three years old. There seemed much time yet. The California coast alone would repay an attentive traveler with many new specimens of plant and earth. Abandoning the great coastal survey of the southern continent, he finally decided to cross Mexico to the Pacific and travel north overland along the West Coast. There were inconveniences . . . a robbery of $100 from one Richardson, who was his house guest, by two young men whom he had befriended and trusted and who escaped on his mules, which they stole. The thieves were caught and jailed, but the money and the mules had been "made away with."

There was a scandal at Chapultepec, too, where Josiah had gone to inspect the historic castle. Questioned by a guard, he answered with asperity. There followed insults, he was jailed, reviled, released, and he made a protest to the United States minister, demanding punishment of the offending officers. Would anything be done? "Nous verrons," he wrote in gloomy sarcasm. He tried, and failed, to meet President Herrera of Mexico. "Mere curiosity," he shrugged. The toll agents on the road in Mexico, of course, betrayed "ill breeding and rascality."

Discovered in a cornfield with his animals and party, Gregg was attacked with excited words by the owner, and only the arrival of the local *alcalde* prevented serious trouble. But Josiah was "unable to believe that the judge was really in good earnest—or it were only a *ruse* to get out of what he considered a bad scrape—Nevertheless, I felt charitable enough to believe the former." Here was Gregg's lack of grace at its worst, or sickest, for his health was gradually leaving him.

On the other hand, his ingenuity and the plains craft taught him so long ago by his frontiersman father were triumphant when his wagon was upset in a wild hinterland, and with nothing but the rude materials at hand, he managed to replace a broken axle, so that the wagon was in even better repair than before. He rolled on toward the west coast of Mexico, full of the idea of Manifest Destiny, in which he "foresaw" Pacific Mexico all occupied by United States citizens down to Mazatlán and even farther south. In this he echoed the popular idea of his time, which seems so foreign to our regard for the independent integrity of the other republics of the hemisphere.

IV

TO
MAD RIVER
AND
THE END

CALIFORNIA

BUT IT WAS A TIME OF EXTRAORDINARY ENER-gies and rumors and news.

What had everyone heard, Gold? In California? First there were exaggerated reports of bonanzas, and then stories of their having given out. —"The placers are said to be failing very much, yet I think it is chiefly owing to the overflowing of the Sacramento river," Gregg decided from Mexico before ever having seen California.

Not feeling really up to a long land journey and knowing what heat and fatigue could do to a toiler on the overland march, he took ship at Mazatlán on July 16, 1849, on the barque *Olga*, for San Francisco. Just before sailing north, it was no surprise to him to discover that Captain Pearson of the S.S. *Oregon*, bound south for Panama, was "unaccommodating"; but how consoling it was to find that Captain Bull of the *Olga* was an admirable ship's master and citizen. As much could not, however, be said for the supercargo of the *Olga*, Mr. Hammersley. But it was a generally pleasant voyage, highlighted by such events as "an agreeable sermon" (July 22) "from a Quaker Universalist on board, the Rev. Mr. Bull" (who was no relation to the captain). At Monterey, where the *Olga* put in briefly, on August 26, there was a delightful, almost reassuring, surprise. He met a

United States paymaster who also botanized. "It is very agree-able to meet with one in thousands who will not permit their ample opportunities to escape, for improving our knowledge of Natural history." At this port, thirty passengers left the ship to proceed to San Francisco on foot, presumably in a great hurry to reach the gold fields.

Aside from the "agreeable and interesting" sermons of the Quaker Universalist, who was a man "of sterling honesty, no doubt, and the best intentions, but of no brilliancy of talent," there were the added diversions of "a company of German min-strels—three lone females, who had wandered from their native land; first to England—then to the U.S.—afterward into Mexico—and now finally on their way to the 'land of golden promise.' They seemed not wholly destitute, as they sustained a character of virtue and unceasing industry." Between the Uni-versalist's unalarming sermons and the conspicuous virtue of the wandering actresses and the appetizing novelty of canned boiled meats from New York, passage on the *Olga* was pleasant; and at last they reached journey's end, and the Golden Gate, which Josiah notes as "decidedly romantic."

CHALLENGE

After that, there was no direct news of him for several months. But in October he was at Rich Bar, where a little community of forty people had gathered on the Trinity River. The rainy sea-son had started; and it snowed as often as it rained. Cloudy mountain barriers lay between this inland settlement and the seacoast. It was wild and remote country, inhabited by scattered Indians on *rancherías*. Yet the Trinity River with its gold placers would one day before long have to have its trade route. Travel overland was not easy or quick, and the mountains forced the route to the south, by inland courses. If a seaport could be found that might serve as the supply center for northwestern California, the country would open up, as they said, ever so much more quickly. What would happen if travelers from here went westward until they reached the ocean? Was there a bay? Would the site support a town? Nobody knew anything but the Indians, and they said there was a bay; but they also said it was almost impossible to reach from here, far up the Trinity, with rain and snow falling every day, and the mountains towering there, and food hard to find.

If they had conceived a challenge for Gregg, they could hardly have made it better.

According to tradition in the Gregg family, Josiah was under government commission to help find the northwestern bay. Twenty-four men at Rich Bar made up the exploring party and elected Gregg captain. But the weather disheartened more of them every day, until only eight in all were left. The Indians tried to discourage the party, saying that the continuous rain here in the valley was snow up in the mountains. But Gregg rarely abandoned a course of action once decided upon; and on November 5, 1849, he led his seven followers up the rainy mountainside. Among them was a young man named L. K. Wood, from Mason County, Kentucky. What happened to them all he never forgot, and many years later wrote an account of the ordeal which contains our only picture of Josiah Gregg in California.

Halfway up the mountain they met the snow. Gregg led them up the steepest slope in order to reach the top more quickly. At nightfall they were there, but to the west lay another wilderness of mountains separating them from the coast they were headed for. In silence they put their blankets on the snow and went to sleep. This first day was the pattern of many that followed. Crossing mountain ridges became almost a hopeless obsession. One night they thought they heard the ocean, and their hopes rose; but the next day they found the swollen waters of the south fork of the Trinity River. Now and then they encountered astonished Indians, who traded them bits of food. Weeks were passing in this search. There came one night when they had no food at all amid the rocks and the pines of the mountains. They spoke of going back. But reason—we may guess whose reason—prevailed, and they went on again in the morning. In the next evening they came hungry to a small high mountain meadow, and during the next few days they found venison. But when it was gone, they toiled through ten days without sight of any game or growth for food. They went through the trees, "this world-wide forest," and now and then found little meadows, where they would rest and hunt, without reward, until one day three of them shot a bear and some deer.

They rarely made over seven miles a day.

But at last the land was changing. The peaks were not so high, although the trees were denser. Any change must presage the country they sought, and their spirits quickened. They calculated that they must be only twelve miles from the sea. The ground was leveling off. They kept some semblance of discipline, which had been worn thin several times before now. They needed it, for now they came into the redwood forests, a prehistoric landscape where nothing but those vegetable giants could be seen. The refuse of centuries lay across their paths and they had to cut their way through it. Their going was slower than ever.

Yet here were matters of interest. "Dr. Gregg frequently expressed a desire to measure the circumference of some of these giants of the forest and occasionally called upon some of us to assist him . . . we not infrequently answered his calls with shameful abuse." Here again is that calm belief in knowledge which was his central concern, even in "this forest prison" where "there was not the least sign indicative of the presence of any of the animal creation," said Wood. Their own pack animals were dying of starvation. Two men went ahead with axes and chopped a system of crude steps up one side of the fallen trees and down the other so the animals could be coaxed onward.

The sounds of the air traveled high in those ancient aisles; and one night, they heard—once again they thought they heard—the "sound of surf rolling and beating upon the shore." They were sure this time; their hearts rose, and the next day three of them went to see, and came back, and sure enough they had seen the Pacific, not over six miles off. At last there it was, the open coast. Once more starving, they separated to hunt. All they could find was an eagle, a raven, and a dead fish, upon which the raven had been feeding. All three were put into the pot for supper. It had taken them over a month to make the journey, though the Indians at Rich Bar had said it would have taken eight days in good traveling weather.

And now that they knew more or less where they were, something seemed to happen among them which released the fears they had not dared give up to before. They had all become increasingly contemptuous of Gregg's scientific attentions to the route. "During our journey over the mountains, the old Doctor took several observations." They derided him for it. Here on the Pacific shore he took observations on a certain plateau, and engraved the latitude and longitude on a nearby tree, "for the benefit," he said, "of those who might hereafter visit the spot, if perchance such an occurrence should ever happen." (A town stands there today.)

It was not long before a collapse of character overtook the whole party. One day "in crossing a deep gulch the Doctor had the misfortune to have two of his mules mire down. He called lustily for assistance, but no one of the company would aid him to rescue them." They had been "annoyed so much," confessed Wood, "and detained so long, in lifting fallen mules . . . that one and all declared they would no longer lend assistance to man or beast, and that from this day forward, each would constitute a company to himself, under obligations to no one and free to act as best suited his notions."

Again, they came to another river, much swollen by recent rains. They made ready to cross it, but Dr Gregg prepared to take observations. The inevitable happened. The others refused to wait for him. They had arranged for canoes with nearby Indians, crossed their possessions, and then made ready to push off by themselves. Only then, Gregg, "as if convinced that we would carry our determination into effect and he be left behind, hastily caught up his instruments and ran for the canoe. He had to wade through the water to catch it." He kept silent while they crossed, but when they reached the opposite bank, his rage escaped him, and he "opened on us a perfect battery of the most withering and violent abuse." He heaped such devastating insults upon the men that some of them moved to pick him up, instruments and all, and throw him to drown in the river. He was sick; these companions constantly spoke of him as an "old man," and "the aged doctor." Yet he was only forty-four. His tenacity must have burned in him with an enabling power to have brought him this far against such obstacles of man and earth. At last, "fortunately for the old gentleman, pacific councils prevailed, and we were soon ready and off again. This stream in commemoration of the difficulty I have just related, we called Mad River," and so it appears on the California map today.

ALLEGORY

This affair (to try and see it from Gregg's view, which is our job) was more than a lot of roughnecks running out on a crank. It was ignorance defying knowledge, and it illustrates how a crisis in relations assumes the shapes of allegory. It was a faith trying to maintain itself amid fear. The scene is ridiculous. The "old man" probably seemed half crazy, a freak, going through abstruse antics with astronomical instruments, offending the body's merit of those strong, younger men. But his qualifying genius kept him at it, and he suffered them, which for a sensitive man was probably torture. He had more to endure than the others; it was their contempt, the sense they gave toward him, of being an old fool, taking all that trouble. He was once again and always the theorist, encountering psychological hardship in the practical world—the essential pattern of Gregg's experience everywhere on the rugged frontier.

Ironically enough, on this day, with its crisis in relations which had made the party forget the object of their search and concentrate their hopes on simply getting away from the wilderness of seacoast where they felt themselves trapped by time and distance, they found a hint of what they had started out to find: one of the men out scouting brought back a sample from "a bay of smooth water." It was dusk, on December 20, 1849, "and was undoubtedly the first discovery of this bay by Americans." They called it Trinity Bay the next morning when they went to see it, and when they left it to go inland, they thought their name secure. But before they could return to civilization to report their find, a party came by sea, headed by "a Captain Douglas Ottinger," who claimed to have discovered it, and he gave it the name of Humboldt Bay, which it bears today. Four considerable towns are on its shores.

And now to get back to the settlements was all they wanted, although they had dreamed of staking claims on the bay and of laying out a city. The eight of them decided to divide into two parties of four men each. The ammunition was nearly gone. They were sick of each other. It was bleak wintertime on the foggy coast. Every scrap they could find to eat meant hours of laborious search. One party of four voted to go eastward, inland. Gregg and his three planned to go down the mountain ridges parallel to the coast until they reached San Francisco. But the mountains defeated them, and at last they, too, turned inland, hoping to come eastward to the Sacramento Valley.

But for one of them, almost any decision would have been all the same. They had no meat; they were living on acorns and herbs; and Gregg, according to one of his last three companions, grew weaker and weaker, though he struggled to go on. But one day—it was in February 1850—"he fell from his horse and died without speaking—died of starvation."

His three companions did what offices were possible. He was buried right there, somewhere near Clear Lake, California.

If Josiah Gregg, in his invariable habit, kept a daily record of his California venture, it did not survive. We know that he "took several observations," to the exasperation of his men. When he died, did he have in his saddlebag the usual small notebooks? Were the men who had treated him so badly exposed in his pages, as he had exposed so many others who had offended him through the years of wandering? When they buried him in the fashion of prairie rites—in a hole dug with sticks, and covered with a cairn of rocks—did they destroy the notebooks which may have contained evidence of their rebellious contempt, which at one point went so far as a threat of murder by drowning? There was, according to John Gregg, some reason to suspect that this was so, though no proof was possible. In any case, no notebooks came back from Clear Lake, and only Wood's later account—oddly candid, since he reported how he and the others had abused their failing captain—remained to tell us the end of Josiah's days.

But Josiah had left in San Francisco a cache of his "memoranda," together with "a work in manuscript, nearly ready for publication," which was the book of his Mexican observations, regarded as lost for nearly a century. These effects, with the news of his death, came back to his home slowly.

THE GRAND COMMUNITY

About a year after Josiah Gregg died, a certain Dr George W. Bayless, to oblige a friend of his who wanted to know the story of Gregg's life, paid a visit to Susannah Gregg, Josiah's mother, and her daughter. What a family. He found the old lady, at seventy-seven, reading "a History of the Reformation in ordinary print." Dr Bayless saw evidence of superior stock in the whole family. The sister and the mother were both "persons of clear good (*strong*) sense." The sister was much like Dr Gregg both physically and mentally, and the old lady's conversation was "marked by clearness and strength." There were nieces and nephews of Josiah visible, and they partook "of the same character." The visitor and Mrs Gregg spoke of the death of her son, and she remarked: "He overtaxed his energies that time."

How often had she seen him come and go. Every time he came back, he could hardly wait to get going again. What had he written John? "I could never live under my oppression of spirits anywhere in the U.S. where I would be liable to continued annoyance."

In his anomalous position among the arch-typical men of his time, Gregg may be taken as an illustration of the man of mind or vision, in a society of movement; but, as such, he may be also a harbinger of our ideal maturity, in which, within our corporate character, as we find individually in his, we may hope to see the freedom of educated men combined with the sense of democratic responsibility. He is among those of our national autobiographers who, simply because they were articulate and honest men, tried with the labors of their lives to make cultural awareness the simple norm of American life. Such early prophets may have been personally lonely men; but there is no loneliness in their work; there is instead a grand community of conviction and enlightenment about the terms of the lives we inherit from them as literature.

Gregg was of the order of men who create literature out of their most daily preoccupations, that is, without a transfiguring act of the imagination. Romantic inaccuracy may produce masterpieces, but so may the earnest magpies, the gossips of fact, they who sense the marvel in the trivial, the whole from the part, and so translate acts of life for us that we come to know ourselves better for knowing them, since their bustling literary acts imply much of larger life itself.

For Gregg said, by implications and acts, that freedom was as desirable as growth—indeed, possibly that they were the same thing; that the prairies were natural domains for America to grow into; that the life of the prairies was beautiful and instructive; that wisdom can be brought to bear upon new experience if conscious observation is an ally; that intelligence is a better mate for courage than simple enthusiasm; and that if a man is alive to the best opinion of his present and aware of his inheritance from the past, then he may perform work valuable to later times.

When Gregg was born in 1806, there was no organized civil life west of the Mississippi. When he died in 1850, four great paths had reached the Pacific. In his short lifetime, forty-four years, the United States achieved its continental design; and he was among the men who helped this to happen.

He might be called the intellectual frontiersman of the natural world. There is high poetry in the quality of his achievement, though its terms at the time never look so. His story is part of a great conquest, in which his particular weapons were curiosity and a batch of little bound books with blank pages, waiting to be written upon.

No chronicler who sought the truth ever needed more.

INDEX